Reading the Ashes

An International Poetry Forum Selection

Reading the Ashes

An Anthology of the Poetry
of Modern Macedonia

Compiled and Edited by

MILNE HOLTON *and* GRAHAM W. REID

UNIVERSITY OF PITTSBURGH PRESS

Published by the University of Pittsburgh Press, Pittsburgh, Pa. 15260
Copyright © 1977, Milne Holton and Graham W. Reid
All rights reserved
Feffer and Simons, Inc., London
Manufactured in the United States of America

Library of Congress Cataloging in Publication Data

Main entry under title:

Reading the ashes.

  (Pitt poetry series)
  1. Macedonian poetry—Translations into English.
2. English poetry—Translations from Macedonian.
I. Holton, Milne. II. Reid, Graham Wightman.
PG1198.E3R4 1977   891.8'19'1   76-41758
ISBN 0-8229-3337-3
ISBN 0-8229-5282-3 (pbk.)

Grateful acknowledgment is made to the editor of the *Macedonian Review* in which many of these translations first appeared.

The following translations are reprinted with permission: "An Ancient Language," "Another City," and "The City at Sunset" from *Modern Poetry in Translation* (England); "Flood at the International Writers' Workshop" and "Professional Poet" from *The Ohio Review* © Carolyn Kizer; "Potter's Song" and "Sleeping Angel" from *Poetry Australia;* "A Green Night in April" and "Peahen" from *Sun & Moon.* "In This Room" first appeared as "In That Room" in *The Christian Science Monitor* © The Christian Science Publishing Society, all rights reserved.

"Anatomy of a Flower," "Ballad of Time," "The City on My Palms," "Drought," "The Evening Ruffled by the Wind," "A Night Without Punctuation," "Poem of a Soldier Six Feet Under," "Prayer for a Simple Word Not Yet Discovered," "Sailor's Song," and "Vij" are reprinted by permission of Vasa D. Mihailovich.

"Journey to the City of Lenguel," "Odysseus in Hell," and "Satanael" were first published by the Ezra Fakir Press.

The publication of this book is supported by a grant from the General Research Board of the University of Maryland.

For SWH and MR

Contents

Contents

Contents

Contents

Contents

Contents

Acknowledgments

We would first thank the students and faculty of the English Seminar at Cyril and Methodius University, Skopje, for their assistance to us in our work on this anthology. Ivanka Koviloska-Poposka of the seminar faculty has encouraged and assisted us from the very inception of the project. Her advice and suggestions have proved invaluable, her encouragement sustaining. Vlado Cvetkovski, also of the seminar faculty, has provided significant assistance; Savé Cvetanovski of the English faculty of the Teachers' College in Skopje has also assisted us in our work. Linda Robinson and her successors among the staff of excellent secretaries in the Department of English, University of Maryland, have shown skill and patience in the typing of the manuscript.

We also wish to express our sincere gratitude to the Honorable Dimčé Belovski, ambassador of Yugoslavia at Washington, a knowledgeable and sincere lover of the poetry of his native republic, and to Dragoljub Budemovski of the Ministry of Information and Culture of Yugoslavia for the encouragement and support they have both given our project. Dr. Anté Rukavina of the Yugoslav-American Binational Commission for Fulbright Affairs has offered us every possible assistance, and the Fulbright-Hays Program has generously supported our work. The Graduate Research Board of the University of Maryland and the International Poetry Forum of the Carnegie Library, Pittsburgh, Pennsylvania, have also been generous in their support of its publication. The Macedonian Writers' Union has offered us full cooperation, advice, and support, and Professor Gané Todorovski of the Writers' Union and of Cyril and Methodius University has made his wide knowledge of Slavic literature available to us.

The successive cultural attachés of the Yugoslav Embassy at Washington who have served during our work on the project, Messrs. Branko Novaković and Dušan Trifunović, have been generous in their assistance. The staffs of the U.S. Information Service, Belgrade, and of the British Council, Belgrade, have been cooperative in every way. Particular mention should be made of the personal interest taken in the project by Mrs. Georgene Lovecky of the Committee for the International Exchange of Persons, Washington, D.C.

There have been certain individuals who have assisted us in the planning and execution of this project, who have recognized from its

Acknowledgments

inception its possibilities and difficulties, and who have been unstinting in their gifts of time and assistance throughout. Without them the completion of our work would not have been possible. In addition to those already mentioned, we would offer special thanks to Professor Vivian D. Pinto of the University of London, and to Elisavietta Ritchie and Eugene Prostov, both of Washington, D.C. Lastly, a special debt of gratitude must be acknowledged to Carolyn Kizer, to Meto Jovanovski, and to Bogomil Gjuzel. These three have been with us all the way.

Introduction

One of the significant but little celebrated results of World War II was the liberation of a language. On July 7, 1945, the tongue of the Macedonian people officially took its place among the European languages. This recognition had been long overdue, for long before the professors and the politicians acknowledged its existence, Macedonian had produced a poetry and a literary tradition. Indeed, the Macedonian poets of the postwar period had not waited for official linguistic recognition but had already begun to publish before 1945.[1] In the thirty years which have followed, this "new" language has increasingly proved itself to be a capable vehicle for the articulation of the poetic imagination. There has in fact been a considerable postwar renaissance in Macedonian poetry, a renaissance which has been one consequence of a long historical process. This process has generated not only a poetry, but a national consciousness among Macedonians, a national consciousness which includes a special and shared imagination among a people whose sad past has too long been submerged in events of greater moment.

Macedonian is today spoken by the southwesternmost of the Slav peoples, who live on the rich Pelagonian plain and in the area drained by the Vardar River. The Vardar, its headwaters in Skopje, the Macedonian capital, flows almost due south into the Aegean at Thessaloniki. A dialect very close to the language of the Macedonians is also spoken by the people living on both slopes of the Pirin Mountains, which separate Macedonia from Bulgaria to her east (the Macedonians today refer to the Bulgarian slope of these mountains as "Pirin Macedonia"). Macedonian, although it has been systematically suppressed in Greece, is nevertheless still spoken by the Slavs living across the Greek border and in the vicinity of Thessaloniki, or Salonika (the Macedonians call the city "Solun" and the region "Aegean Macedonia").

Macedonia is today a socialist republic, the southernmost of the six which comprise modern Yugoslavia. But it has not always been so.

---

1. Aco Šopov's *Pesni* ("Poems") was published in 1944. See Blagoja Korubin, "The Formation of the Macedonian Literary Language," *Macedonian Review* I (1971), 54—71.

Introduction

Indeed, almost since the coming of the Slavs to the area in the sixth century A.D., the Macedonian plains have been a rich prize eagerly sought after by stronger and more aggressive neighbors, the traditional spoil in the long and bloody history of Balkan political and military struggle. This fact has determined the development and the direction of her poetry.

The history of the language—at least in its written form—had its beginnings when, in the ninth century A.D., Cyril, a Byzantine monk from the city of Salonika, created an alphabet in preparation for the proselytizing of the Moravian Slavs. There were many Slavs in Cyril's own city, and their speech provided him with the language upon which he could base the orthography of what was later to be known as Old Church Slavonic. Thus, Macedonian philologists today claim that their language in an early state is the source for the oldest of the written Slavic languages.

The Slavs of this region, however, did not produce a written literature until much later. Even from the Middle Ages, a period of great cultural splendor for the peoples of the southern Balkans, the time when Cyril's student, Clement, founded a monastic university on the shores of Lake Ohrid, the time when those jewellike churches which dot the Macedonian, Serbian, and Bulgarian countryside were built, and the time of the development of a theological literature in Old Church Slavonic on Lake Ohrid, there has survived no vernacular literature of note in Macedonia. And when, in 1389 at Kosovo on the Plain of the Blackbirds, Tsar Lazar's army was destroyed by the Ottomans, and the brilliance of the old Serbian empire of the Nemanjan dynasty was extinguished, the Macedonians were also soon to fall under the Turkish yoke, which they would bear for five hundred years.

So there was to be no Renaissance, no Reformation, no Enlightenment in this region—no new birth of humanism in which a vernacular literature could grow and flourish. For the next four hundred years the culture of the Slavs of the southern Balkans consisted of a struggle for the preservation of the memory of a past time. Then the Slav poets of the region composed their didactic *damaskini*. And they sang to their audiences the dark epic poems of the Battle of Kosovo and the narratives of a legendary despot from Prilep named Marko (Marko kralé), whose struggles against the sultan were recounted in poems also absorbing the legends of the Thracian horseman, of St. George, and even of Stefan Dušan, the greatest of the Nemanjan kings.

It is in these songs that the Macedonian poets today find the sources of their poetry. But if continuity is a necessary element in tradition, there is certainly no "tradition" of poetry in Macedonia. It was not until well into the nineteenth century that those beginnings came to be recognized as of immediate relevance. This recognition came at first in the form of a kind of ethnic renaissance of Macedonian and Bulgarian self-awareness, a movement no doubt inspired by the example of the Croatian Slavophile and nationalist, Bishop Strossmayer of Zagreb. In the southern Balkans the imperial master was not the Austrian, but the Ottoman Turk, with his Greek agents; nevertheless these southern Slavs also developed an awareness of the value of their own languages and traditions and felt the impulse to establish that tradition in literature. In Bulgaria there occurred what Professor Pinto has identified as a "national renaissance," a *preporod*.[2] In Macedonia, at Ohrid, this awareness took its first form in the collection of Macedonian folk songs by Dimitar and Konstantin Milandinov; the work was undertaken at the suggestion of Grigorović, the Russian Slavist who was visiting Ohrid in 1845. Dimitar Miladinov also began (but never published) a first grammar of the Macedonian language. But it was his brother, Konstantin, who was Macedonia's first poet of modern times.

The Miladinovs were rewarded for their work by imprisonment; they died in a Turkish prison in Istanbul in 1862.[3] But in the latter half of the nineteenth century there were others of like sentiment. Many were to study in Russia and were there to increase their awareness of their share in the Slavic heritage. Partenija Zografski was one; his awareness led him to question the propriety of Bulgarian as the literary language

---

2. Vivian Pinto, ed., *Bulgarian Prose and Verse* (London: The Athlone Press, 1957), p. xiii, uses the Bulgarian word *vazradane* to describe a similar event in that country.

3. The collection of folk songs was published in Zagreb in 1861. See Pinto, p. xviii, n. 6, and Korubin, p. 55.

for Macedonians. Another was the poet-journalist Rajko Žinzifov, and Bishop Zografski's most noted follower, Kuzman Šapkarev.

Macedonians today, however, look to Grigor Prličev as the outstanding figure in the establishment of their modern poetry. Prličev, who was born in Ohrid in 1830 or 1831 and taught for a time in Tirana (Albania), made his first reputation in Athens in 1860 as a Greek university poet. But the tragedy of the Miladinovs convinced him to return to his native Ohrid, to live among his own people, and to write—not in Greek—but in "Pan-Slavonic," a kind of Slavonic Esperanto of his own creation which he hoped would serve as a literary language uniting the South Slavs. He translated the *Iliad* and his own epics, *The Sirdar* and *Scanderbeg* into his "Pan-Slavonic," and he even attempted a grammar of the language, but he was never able to attain the level of poetry in this as yet unestablished literary language that he had achieved in Greek. As Prličev himself admitted, he, who had sung like a swan in Greek, must now cry like an owl in Slavonic. But his struggle—in the face of attacks by Bulgarian critics—to produce a poetry that would establish a literary language, and his solid achievement of a remarkable autobiography written entirely in his native language, have made for him a place in the consciousness of Macedonians today as a father of their poetry.

Unfortunately, the last decades of the nineteenth century were hardly conducive to the development of a literary tradition. They were, instead, years of violence and struggle which began with the cruel repression of the April Rising in Bulgaria in 1876 and saw the liberation of Bulgaria in 1878 and the Bulgaro-Serbian war in 1885, a war in which Macedonia was to be the prize for the victor. These were the years in which Gladstone's cry of 1897, "Macedonia for the Macedonians," would go unheeded, years of the barbarities and violent reprisals of the Vrhovisti, agents of the Bulgarian monarchy, of *Komiti* and of terror. In 1903, at Kruševo on Ilinden (St. Ilija's Day), Macedonian revolutionaries declared the establishment of an idealistic socialist republic which, had it survived, might well have been a key to the solution of Balkan problems. It lasted for eleven days. At the end of that same year, when Krsté Misirkov had the temerity again to assert the possibility of autonomy for the Macedonian language and people in a book printed in Sofia, the book was suppressed, and Misirkov was savagely beaten by Bulgarian sympathizers and forced to flee to Russia for his life.[4]

Thus, in the early years of the twentieth century, when Turkish domination gradually receded and under Ataturk was finally withdrawn, the Macedonians' former brothers in the long struggle for Slavic self-realization in the Balkans—the Serbs and the Bulgarians—became competitors for the role of their new master. Macedonia was again the prize for the antagonists in the First Balkan War, which broke out in 1912. During World War I she provided the road for the Serbian army's long retreat, then the battleground to make the army's triumphant return to Belgrade possible. And after that war (and yet another Balkan War) Macedonia was partitioned—among Bulgaria, Greece, and the new, Serbian-dominated Yugoslav kingdom.

So the last decades of the nineteenth century and the opening decades of the twentieth were not years of cultural self-realization for the Macedonians. Indeed, it was then usually illegal and certainly physically dangerous even to teach Macedonian in Macedonian schools. These were hardly conditions under which a Macedonian poetry could flourish. It seemed that the brief period of stirrings toward a Macedonian literature were over; the birth of the new poetry had been a stillbirth.

Such an interpretation, however, does not take into account what was to happen after World War II—or what was beginning to happen even in the thirties. For it was in the 1930s that Kosta Solev Racin again began to write poetry in Macedonian and again asserted the autonomy of Macedonian as a literary language. Other poets writing in Macedonian as well were beginning to appear in print—Kolé Nedelkovski and Vapcarov and Markovski—along with a number of dramatists. There was even—illegally printed—a Macedonian newspaper.

Kosta Racin died with the partizans in the war, but when Macedonia was liberated by those partizans in 1944, it was Macedonian—regularized from those central dialects identified as Macedonian by Misirkov in

---

4. See Korubin, p. 59.

xxi

1903 in his suppressed book—which became the official language, the language of her government and of her schools and of her university at Skopje.[5] And that long-awaited legitimation of a language was ratified by poetry. Almost immediately, in the very same year, one of Macedonia's most distinguished modern poets, Aco Šopov, published *Pesni* ("Poems"), the first postwar collection of Macedonian verse.

It is the work of Šopov and the poets who followed him in the generations after the war which is at the center of our collection. As will be apparent, this poetry in its brief postwar history has developed rapidly, and in a surprisingly varied number of directions. A first and perhaps an easiest direction to anticipate might be that of affirmation—affirmation of the links with a past both regional and ethnic, a past whereby the Macedonian can identify himself in space and in time and in racial awareness. Blaže Koneski, whose work as an historical linguist has established him as the immediate father of the modern Macedonian language, is also often regarded as the founder of her modern poetry. In poems like "Vij" we see Koneski reach back in memory to search out those symbols which are shared in the unconscious of all Macedonian people. It is therefore, perhaps, not surprising that Koneski has, among his other activities, translated the poetry of the Russian symbolist, Aleksandr Blok.

The other anticipated direction of postwar Macedonian poetry must, of course, be that of social commitment. Certainly Kosta (or "Kočo," the affectionate diminutive by which he is usually identified) Racin stands at the beginning of this movement. But even though he is much adulated, it is remarkable that his example has not been widely followed, at least not since 1948. Probably Anté Popovski's "S. F. R. J." (which is not included here) and his "Macedonia" (which is excerpted) are unique examples. For among Macedonian—indeed, among Yugoslavian—poets there is little evidence of much of a taste for "social realism." There was in the first place very little enforcement of social realism as a critical doctrine anywhere in Yugoslavia, and this is especially true since Tito's break with Stalin in 1948. Since that time, Party

---

5. See Korubin, p. 60.

control of literature in Yugoslavia has become very much the exception rather than the rule, the act of creative expression has come to be separated in the minds of most intellectuals from the political act, and since the early fifties most of the Macedonian poets have made no effort to write a socially committed poetry.

Indeed, many Macedonian poets—quite early on—came to find themselves deeply committed to another kind of realism, a private honesty and frankness which at times seems to border upon what Americans call "confessional" poetry. Gané Todorovski is recognized for this characteristic in his poetry. This impulse toward intense and private expression is also apparent in the unusually distinguished and somewhat younger poet, Bogomil Gjuzel, whose recent work has begun to generate both the symbolic power of Koneski and the private intensities of Todorovski.

Another direction apparent in the poetry since the war has been the result of a rather radical social transition which has been the experience of many Macedonians. Macedonia, probably one of the last overwhelmingly village cultures in Europe at the end of the Second World War, has experienced a movement of population from the village to the city which is probably unequalled anywhere in the west. Skopje, rebuilt since its terrible earthquake in 1963, is now a modern city swollen with people, while many villages are emptied of all but the very old. Thus it is not surprising to see the development of a perhaps slightly retrospective pastoral poetry, a poetry filled with the imagery of the rural beauty left behind, and—more particularly—a poetry enriched by the primitive vitality of images etched in the walls of the unconscious of such poets of peasant stock come to the city as Radovan Pavlovski. And, since there is almost no Macedonian today without his kinsmen in the villages, such imagery is surely to be found almost everywhere—in the poems of Todorovski and Koneski and Popovski as well.

Yet, if Macedonian poetry is a poetry rooted deeply in soil and climate,[6] it also turns outward for vitality and strength. From Koneski onward, Macedonian poets have reflected the influences on European

---

6. See Graham W. Reid, "Differences of Soil and Climate: Poetry in Macedonia," *Macedonian Review* II (1972), 230–35.

Introduction

poetry from both east and west. Vlada Urošević is perhaps the most frequently noted example; he had his beginning in surrealist experiments, in "automatic writing," and the humor apparent in his verse has an absurdist quality which puts us in mind of Eugene Ionesco and his Rumanian disciple, Marin Sorescu. Mateja Matevski has translated the work of Apollinaire and Lorca, and his own poetry reflects the spirit of the modern French and perhaps a darker Spanish influence. Bogomil Gjuzel's early poetry ("Troy" is an example) reflects his period of study in Britain and the influence of T. S. Eliot and Edwin Muir. So the poetry of modern Macedonia, engaged as it is in its own history, myth, and soil, is yet a part of a larger community of the imagination.

The thirty years of poetry of postwar Macedonian have been enough to demonstrate the remarkable range of potential in her poets. These years have also begun to show the historical growth and development of her poetry. Accordingly, we have arranged the poems presented in this collection in four sections and an appendix: the appendix to set forth something of the topography of a shared literary consciousness, the four sections to demonstrate the process of development in the poetry since World War II. This arrangement of the postwar poetry, grouped as it is according to generations, should not suggest that any spirit of antagonism exists between literary fathers and children in Macedonia, for indeed the writers there are remarkably free of such antagonisms. Rather, our intention has been to give some sense of the chronological flow which inevitably begins to describe historical sequence, even in a poetry whose tradition cannot be traced continuously beyond fifty years.

The first section of the collection is devoted to those three poets who burst into prominence in the years just following the Liberation. Here is Blaže Koneski, a reflective and scholarly poet drawing from his own experiences in his own culture and from the poetry of the other Slav peoples. Slavko Janevski, perhaps Macedonia's most prolific writer, is the partizan poet who survived, whose simple, lonely, ironic, and vivid imagination makes his poems still very much alive. Lastly, here we have the poetry of Aco Šopov, complex, profound, and deeply private, and perhaps of the three the richest and most sharply influential upon those who followed.

Introduction

The poets in the section which follows, "The Middle Generation," manifest a commitment to the sharpening of sensibilities, the broadening of intellectual range, and the sophistication of technique which shaped the work of many artists elsewhere in Europe as well as in Macedonia, who were members of that generation educated in the first stable years following the war. The poets of the middle generation went about the work of developing a tradition from what had gone before. Among them are to be found the brilliant lyricist, Srbo Ivanovski, Anté Popovski, who may well prove to be the last of the really nationalist poets, the romantic Mateja Matevski, and Gané Todorovski, the brilliant technician whose remarkable self-awareness would place him at the forefront of any generation of poets.

In the early 1960s, however, a number of Macedonian poets began to look in new directions. Some of them turned away from the sources of imagination found in their native region to seek out the mainstreams of the European poetic tradition. Others reached ever more downward to seek fresh sources in their own mythic past. Because of their impulses toward fresh discoveries, we have grouped a number of poets, all of them born in the early 1930s, in the section labeled "The New Poets." In this section will be found the poems of the ironic and sophisticated modernist, Vlada Urošević, of Petar Boškovski with his dark and violent imagination, and of the unique and charismatic Radovan Pavlovski, who, because of his unclassifiable imagination and his impact upon present-day readers, could as well have been placed in the next section with Gjuzel and the "Avant-Garde" poets of the 1970s.

The final section begins with the poems of Bogomil Gjuzel, a poet who has made a journey very much his own in his search for the origins of deep psychic impulses as they are embodied in the mythologies of Slav peoples. The section also includes a younger generation of Macedonian poets, poets still in their twenties and thirties, led by Gjuzel, Pavlovski, and the remarkable lyricist, Atanas Vangelov. These younger poets seem to be manifesting new impulses—toward a new incisiveness and compression, toward a new simplicity of emotion, toward new firmness and vitality of language. It may be that these impulses can characterize the poetry being written in Macedonia just now.

From reading these, especially such poets as Blaže Koneski and

Introduction

Bogomil Gjuzel, it will be immediately apparent that this newest of European literatures is almost obsessively aware of its roots in a literary past that is at least several hundred years old and its inheritance of a mythology with its origins in a pre-Christian imagination. Thus we have appended, in a final section entitled "Ancestors," a handful of examples of the richness of the tradition of Macedonian oral poetry and a few poems chosen from the most important written in that language during the period of the long struggle for cultural autonomy which reached its successful conclusion in 1945. It is to be hoped that the poems collected in this section will provide a suggestion of the shape of the collective literary memory of the poets whose work has been presented in the previous sections. It is a memory of a nationalist tradition, a tradition of folk songs celebrating the beauty of women, telling stories of death and loss in battle, and providing people with heroes, now in sickness but soon to return to vindictive vigor, heroes like Marko kralé and Dojčin, heroes who embody hope. These narrative and epic poems patterned the memory which served in Macedonia, as elsewhere in the Balkans, for many years in the place of a recorded history.

There are more genres of traditional poetry than there is space in the Appendix to represent them. Notable among those omitted are the sad songs of the emigrants who remember the beauty of a homeland far away; Macedonia, like Ireland, has long been and is still a land of emigration. One may hear only echoes of these songs in Konstantin Miladinov's "Longing for the South," a poem itself written from a long exile, which is included in this section. Also to be found in this first section is one poem of Grigor Prličev, whom the poets in Macedonia today still recognize as their tragic progenitor. And also here is the socially committed poetry of Kosta Racin, who holds a place, still not surely defined, in the affection of the contemporaries.

Any collection of poetry written by a number of people who have lived in a particular time and in a particular place is, in a sense, a record of a sharing of experience and consciousness, and this collection makes that claim and no other. It is not conceived as evidence for an argument concerning linguistic autonomy, and it should not be construed as such. But it does assert a claim which moves very much in the direction of an assertion of literary autonomy. At least we stand behind our suggestion that a significant number of, we believe, quite significant writers living and writing in a particular corner of the world, are full members as well of the literary generations who have written elsewhere in Europe and in the Americas since the Second World War. Also, we believe, this group of Balkan poets have shared a defining awareness and a shaping vision. We wish the poems that follow to stand as evidence for these claims.

MILNE HOLTON

College Park, 1976

A Note on the Pronunciation of Macedonian Names

Although the Macedonian language is written in the Cyrillic alphabet, proper names are set here in the Latin alphabet and are spelled as they would be in Croatian. Like Macedonian and Serbian, Croatian is basically spelled as it is pronounced, one symbol representing one sound. But sometimes letters are used two or three times, with differing diacritical marks to indicate that they are being used for differing sounds. Most letters have sounds equivalent to their sound in English. Set forth below are approximate sounds for other letters.

c	ts
ć	as in 'cure'
č	ch
g	hard, as in English 'go'
j	y (consonant)
š	sh
ž	zh
dž	soft, as in the initial g in 'George'
gj	as in 'ague'
h	ch as in 'Bach'

Generally Macedonian is distinguished from the other Yugoslav languages in its permanent accent on the antepenultimate (third from the last) syllable. In two-syllable names, the accent falls on the first syllable.

MH *and* GWR

A Note on the Translations

We first conceived of the idea of compiling and translating the poetry of modern Macedonia in 1970, when we were both teaching in the English Seminar at Cyril and Methodius University, Skopje. We recognized from the outset that, because the Macedonian language was young and linguistically volatile, there would be few people fluent in both languages who could assist us in the work of translation. Indeed, there are few enough people fluent in both English and Macedonian as it is spoken today, and of those even fewer possess a reading experience and sophistication of prosodic knowledge sufficient for rendering competent translations of poetry into English.

Thus we decided that the process of translation was to be threefold. First, a rendering into English of the Macedonian poem would be undertaken by a bilingual translator. Secondly, this translation would be "reworked" by a person familiar both with the techniques and conventions of modern poetry in English and with the problems of verse translation. In some cases, of course—indeed in a rather large number—the original rendering would prove to be acceptable without further change. In others, however, changes had to be considered in order that a clear and unambiguous sense of the meaning of the original Macedonian poem be transmitted to English readers. In a few cases, considerations of aesthetic norms and of connotative ambiguities caused these secondary translators (many of whom are themselves poets) to make significant changes in the original renderings—changes which went beyond word choice to alterations of the syntax or imagery of the original. It was agreed that in these cases the use of the term "translation" might create a false impression. Thus we agreed to label these secondary translations "imitations" (and in one case of extreme reduction, "rendering"). But in every case, the final result was closely examined by a bilingual reader as a third step in the translation process, to make sure that the final version still conveyed as faithfully as possible the sense of the whole poem as it was originally presented in Macedonian.

At the end of each poem the translator, often more than one, is indicated. When more than one name appears, the order of their appearance indicates the role each played in the translation process of that poem. The first person mentioned was involved in the shaping of

A Note on the Translations

the final translation or imitation and was thus the closest to the English version. The last named was responsible for the first transmission of the poem from Macedonian into English and was thus closest to the original Macedonian poem.

In a number of cases translators have begun by working from intermediate translations—either French translations from Gaucheron and Albertini's *La Poésie Macédonienne* (Paris: ERF, 1972) or English versions of Macedonian poems which appeared in Giorgio Nurigiani's *Macedonia Yesterday and Today* (Rome: Teleuropa, 1967) and elsewhere. In each case, the final translation has been carefully compared with the original to establish conformity. And, since even those translations from English intermediates represent substantial departures from the intermediates, the use of the intermediate has not been noted.

Any translation of poem is at best a rough approximation of its original, and each pairing of languages for purposes of translation presents its own peculiar problems. It is our hope that the translations in this anthology succeed in providing that approximation, that the procedure outlined above has yielded results which are acceptable themselves as poems and which bear adequate fidelity to their Macedonian originals.

MH *and* GWR

I
The Establishment

BLAŽÉ KONESKI

Bolen Dojčin

When I was full of a power
which rose
        as the troubled headwaters of the river,
when I felt myself ready for exploits
        worthy of glory,
when my voice was tested by the deepest word,
my hand by the heaviest sword,
my foot by the truest step,
I broke.
I fell as a branch of the cherry tree snaps
        under the weight of so much fruit,

A mocking shadow followed me relentlessly,
        as the snake in the hole in the tomb
        glides through my soul,
cast a spell over my laughter,
cloaked my sadness in black,
I was devoured by suspicion,
terrified that I had strayed.

Then I felt myself small, grotesque, base.
My body, soft.
My arms, liquid.
The sword fell from my hand
and I fell in sickness.

"Bolen Dojčin" ("Sick Dojčin," or "Dojčin the Ill One") refers by its title to one of the oldest of the Macedonian narrative poems, a translation of which is included in the Appendix. The old oral narrative, probably first composed some five hundred years ago, has come to represent the very embodiment of their tradition for a number of modern Macedonian poets, Blažé Koneski and Bogomil Gjuzel among them. It tells the story of a bedridden warrior of Salonika (whom many regard as originally a Macedonian city), who rises from his sickbed to defeat "the Black Arab" (The Turkish oppressor) and then to avenge his sister's honor. The modern poets draw ironic allusion to the original and see in Dojčin's illness a parallel to their modern condition. Cf. also Gjuzel's "Bolen Dojčin." ED.

3

I have been ill nine years.
I have used nine beds.

I cannot feel my knees,
I have been spilled out on the parched heath,
on the sunbaked ridge at midday,
my bones disconnected at the joints.
Inside my limbs, grass is growing.
In that grass, snakes hatch.

I thirst for a cool, quiet tomb,
but this will not end
until I achieve what I am fated to do.

Unknown woman, unique woman,
my sister and my mother,
you who have suffered everything,
languishing in almost petrifying tortures,
come, my golden sister,
reassemble my watery bones. Without disgust,
put me back together.
Wrap me in three hundred cubits of cloth.
Comfort me with your words.
Raise me up,
teach me again to walk, mother,
give me a sword
to kill the Black Arab.

To die.

translation by Edward Gold

BLAŽE KONESKI

Vij

I have locked you in my consciousness as in
a midnight church. And as candles fade
toward the end, you now grow pale,
and all the saints follow you lustfully.
You are here a captive for whom
I am making so many solemn vows,
and the hour is already approaching
and everything points to my revelation.
I come like that terrible Vij,
eyes gray, all of me a thirsty earth,
yes, I am terrible, and because I bring tenderness
in hard clumps—you are pale.
I approach as tender Vij, but already
you have drawn the mysterious line,
and as soon as I reach that spot, suddenly
the precipice tumbles down and rock crushes rock.
And like thirsty sand, I slide
into that abyss, and fade away.
I, Vij, lured you mightily into my consciousness,
but, thirsty, have no strength to reach you.

translation by Vasa D. Mihailovich

According to Nicolai Gogol, who makes use of the legend in one of his
fantastic tales, Vij is a leader of the gnomes, whose heavy eyelids reach the
ground. If his eyes are exposed, his glance petrifies, like the basilisk's. Gogol
identifies the legend as Ukrainian, but Vij also appears in Serbian and Macedonian
mythology as a god of the lightning, whose glance can reduce men and towns to
ashes. ED.

5

BLAŽÉ KONESKI

Coal

If I just close my eyes
coal grows out of the dirt,
eyeless old men, black and worried,
rise up to me,
their harsh brows and wrinkles
come near my face.
If I press my eyelids hard—
black, the coal piles into rock,
and grows up over me
and covers me
and grinds and mixes me
until I'm a black lump
in an underground mine,
a black stone which whispers
I can burn.

imitation by Roland Flint from a translation by Ivanka Koviloska-Poposka

6

BLAŽE KONESKI

Sterna

But my old folks, are they not afraid of the Sterna of Prince
Marko below Marko's Towers; Marko who checked the water
with goodness knows how many sacks of cotton and hammered
nails as long as an ell so that the water was enclosed and the
plain of Prilep saved from becoming another Lake of Ohrid.

M. Cepenkov

I stopped the Sterna with cotton,
with rags,
with sand, with gravel,
with stones and rocks
which I piled into the crack
that they would hold.

It was the last moment!

My sleep had vanished.
At an ungodly hour
I went to listen to the approaching water
gurgling and rumbling and groaning underground
angry with someone—
but its speech was not to be understood—
it was getting ready to come out,
like a gray bear from its cave,
to go on the hunt.

Night.

I knew: patiently
it bides its time.

Prince Marko (kraljević Marko), or King Marko (Marko kralé) as he is known to most Macedonians, was a historical figure who has become a legendary hero to the Slavs of the southern Balkans. Historically he was a brigand lord and a simple vassal of the Ottomans who lived in and around Prilep between 1325 and 1394. In legend, and in poetry, however, Prince Marko has become a hero of grand and sometimes comic dimensions, a Paul Bunyan-like figure, who personifies not only the virtues of the Thracian horseman of pagan and the St. George of Christian art, but the manly virtues of strength and heroism and the deeply felt need for a champion against oppression which has been for so long an integral part of the

It will wait for the mother to lull her child to sleep
and the cradle to cease rocking,
for the windlass to stop turning;
it will wait for the ploughmen
to unwind their footcloths,
to stuff their shoes with straw;
it will wait for the last ember to go out
underneath the ash,
for the last bell in the sheepfold to fall silent,
for the birds to quiet down
and for the old people troubled by sleeplessness and coughing
to become still.
So that it is a deaf and peaceful and dark time when it roars.
The Sterna,
It is but biding its time.

All are asleep,
and only I awake in the pregnant night
like an outlaw in an ambush,
waiting,
full of its subterranean sound
my very flesh creeping when for a while it is calm
for then it hesitates, planning the worst.
I feel like shouting, waving my arms, rousing the people!

And then I made up my mind:

Macedonian imagination. The real Marko was a loyal vassal of the Turks, albeit a benevolent and strong ruler; the legendary Marko is a rebel against oppression and a protector and benefactor of the common people.

Marko has given rise to the veritable cycle of heroic poetry—the poetry of the Serbs, Bulgarians, and Croats, the Albanians, Rumanians, and Slovenes, as well as the Macedonians. In it Marko, and his fabulous horse, are of superhuman strength and intelligence. One of Marko's feats was the damming of the Sterna, a spring which lay at the foot of the hill on which stands his fortress, overlooking the plain before Prilep.

One of the folk poems of the Marko cycle, not so much a heroic poem as a comic one, is included in the Appendix. ED.

I stopped the Sterna with cotton,
with rags,
with sand, with gravel
with stones and rocks
which I piled into the crack
that they would hold.

How I rejoiced
that I had strangled it to mortal collapse,
that its voice came ever softer
from underground
as if it sobbed, seeking mercy.

I gathered strength, torn by rage,
with my nails, uprooting, flailing, beating,
crumbling and heaping up a great mass.
I hurried lest I should melt to its voice.
And when I stood up, breathless and sweating,
and passed my muddied hand across my brow,
when I stretched upright,
inhaling with my whole heart fresh air and silence,
I heard
something below the soil chuckling far off
as if it covered its mouth with its hand.

I stiffened.

And now again it is night and an ungodly hour.
All are asleep, but sleep is lost to me.
The Sterna sounds in my ears like never before
as if it were all poured into me
here in my breast
and in my temples;
the dark underground waters draw near
without stopping
as if I had created the Sterna
and must mouth its speech.
I listen

9

while it grows.
It is but biding its time
so that it is a deaf and peaceful and dark time when it roars,
when it gushes forth,
when it bursts out, covers, sinks, and retreats,
when it comes to rest in this great expanse.

translation by Graham W. Reid

Drowsiness

This strange drowsiness—
Sleepy and satisfied—
While your body still burns,
Tries to reproach me.
Your dreams at night are simple,
Girl wholly in love:
I'd say every evening you pick
A ripe apple from the branch.
How can I thank you? I burn
With a different longing.
The wish to retell it
is frozen in me.

translation by Roland Flint

BLAŽÉ KONESKI

A Child Sleeping by the Lake

While you are sleeping
the lake is musing,
preparing your life.
You can't hear it splashing a little,
entering you.
Like a small bay where
sometimes each white pebble can be seen.
You are sleeping
but the smallest ripple now
leads like a thread to those loud waves,
which cry and will take you along.
Sleep, child—
the lake is arranging you
and how your future stirs.

imitation by Roland Flint from a translation by Ivanka Koviloska-Poposka

Cage

Thirty years. And what's done?
Thirty broken urns.
The child's imprisoned in me.
In a cage of wrinkled burns.

translation by Ivanka Koviloska-Poposka

The Poem of a Soldier Six Feet Under

I am no more.
The sinews of my throat
remained on the bellflowers.
In the twilight the winds
lie on them.
                    Good night, birds.

I am no more.
The darkness of my eyes
remained on dark blue waters.
In the twilight the whirlpools
drink them thirstily.
                    Good night, fogs.

I am no more.
The fingers of my hands
remained under the grass.
In the twilight girls gather
flowers.
                    Good night, nights.

I am no more, no more.

The sinews vibrate in pain:
"Olive-tree, hold up the sky,
so it won't fall down."
The eyes burst from water:
"Let branches sprout from us,
we come from your seed."
The fingers beg the grass:
"Wrap us in your bark, tree,
the frost is hurting us."

I am no more . . .

On my forehead lies
a good night
a heavy night
a long night.

translation by Vasa D. Mihailovich

A Green Night in April

A green visitor came tonight—do you hear?—green to his root;
he came without "hello," without "here I am" or "I am coming,"
he came green as the sea,
with green milk in his veins, with a green bite in his teeth,
he came like a green bird under old eaves,
this green guest with a green laugh,
this restless one, green from gorge to forehead;
he came—you hear? He whispered, "I've come green:
if death comes all in white, I come like rain,
like April, like the light,"
he whispered, "like a dream, like time, like deer."

And he came with that whisper—did you hear?
"Let everything be green tonight," it said,
"the songs of all the roosters," so it said,
"the loves of all the grasses," so it said,
"the sadness of the waters," so it said;
"green, green, let everything be green," it said,
"everything born, and everything to come."

A green visitor came tonight, and I saw him;
the wind was a green rider,
a drunk beggar with a peg leg,
a vagabond, a child above children,
a green girl with green hair
and a green moon, a horny goat
with a green flag from each horn.

13

I saw, you know, something I've never seen,
something really thirsty—for thirst, for drink;
I saw the green guest come through this town,
I saw him—you hear?

translation by Milne Holton and Vasa D. Mihailovich

Veins

Rip them out in anger at the past,
weave them with fury for the future,
and call them the scourge of time.

Then begin:
scourge the lovers
who found five continents of their world
in a five-leaf clover,
and those deep sleepers
who take dangerous journeys—like Icarus—
and the architects with hollow cheeks
who lie exhausted behind their dream of tresses.

When you've done, my love,
make a noose of those veins
and put it around my neck;
hanged from a star's tail
my feet will touch the sea of sleepwalkers,
I will dry out in dead typhoons.

Promise you'll do it.
Then I, or someone like me,
can claim credit for all the lovers,
for the leaps across time,
for the towers with the blue cranes' nests.
Do it, and when you see me hanging there,

14

with your Eve's cunning say to them:
"So that's all you are, you veins,
Only strings of blood."

translation by Herbert Kuhner, Milne Holton, and Graham W. Reid

Dancer on a Palm

No single smith will forge you any more,
not even from gold.
So wide and strong,
this unresting palm
with spears whose name is longing
with a hyacinth which sets traps for the sun,
no one will weave for you
neither from any restlessness
nor from felt pain. For my pain is the only pain,
and every joint has its own secret.
In one, winds flay my skin,
in another wolves pull out sinews from my heels,
in a third sleeplessness awaits me with its spear.

Don't be afraid, come,
there is everything in these joints:
the nadir of things. Listen.
They offer you dark unbeings;
in my laughing
they raise bloody towers to the suns;
my waiting under them
fans evil fires.
That burning waits, waits for you
to burn up, to perish, or to grow
to a black memory.

15

Come, we belong to each other, I to hunger,
and you to a reproach; what we both are
we are to the roots.
Why is it that I desire you so winnowy,
so that my joints don't ache
from your dance,
from the embroidery you leave
behind your white steps?
If my skin is hard,
stretch it out and beat it,
one dances softer on bare flesh,
fair-haired one.
Dance, drunk from my blood,
and don't be angry with my eyes
for the way they are, reading you naked as the dawn.
Look, look, rye gave birth to you, whiteness,
I listen to the rattle of spears under your skin;
red-sunned raspberries have nourished you,
endless sounds quiver in your eyelashes;
south winds, like bandits, have lulled you to sleep,
and your skin covers me completely.

But what is that, that golden moon
below your unwept throat?
I forgot: from struggling with wild boars and jackals
my jaw is firmer than the law,
and when these lips burn,
love raises an itch on my lips.

Dance, dance your fill,
warm my skin with your leaps,
the ice has left my red joints
and now, now, now
the longing in them fears death.
I will burn, burn.
When I leave my ash on the stone,
write your name on it;

for the winds and wild boars to carry it off
in all directions.
Then go on with your embroidery of dance,
with your insatiable whisper.
Palm, my friend, where are you,
where are you, green apple?

translation by Milne Holton, Vasa D. Mihailovich, and Graham W. Reid

Peahen

It bears day under its wing
drop of song on its peak
untold dreams in the eyes . . .

Four peacocks were tearing each other with screams
blood and love spitting from them.

Four—
and when the elm leaned over them
he saw red streams
dead wings
and eyes hungry for love.

It bears darkness under its wing
hunger and sorrow on its beak
dumb grace in its eyes.

Bird, does it hurt to have love—
and a lifeless wing?

translation by Roland Flint

SLAVKO JANEVSKI

Intimately
For Šopov

When I heard your pain, the cry for your son,
I saw you stopped somewhere, as if listening.
When I thought of the wrongs you have known,
You were in me, suffering.

I remember, and see our days;
We knew blades of the same grass,
In the hayloft one dawn our song sprang from fear,
Rough, from clumsy hands.

We were like recruits before the first battle.
I'd like to embark from there again, in that same laughter,
To hear it shouting through the woods, you drunk on poetry and wine,
To hear the woods breathe, to find you hugged by your son.

Let it be as it was then, the boy kissing your white face
And simply saying to you,
Father who lights and hangs the sun?
And let it be that dreams of stories made him sleep

As easily as they did my son.
Let his whisper baffle you easily.
I want to see the Red Ridinghood.
But in the hurry, in the close hug of the day,

A son will go to school, and his thumb will tremble
A page petrified in all that pain,
Woven from the warm thread of a father's words.
Don't be surprised if the boy's sadness flattens the sun's disc.

The occasion for this poem is the death of the son of Janevski's friend and
fellow poet, Aco Šopov. ED.

SLAVKO JANEVSKI

Tonight a plain song asking forgiveness
Has caught me in its strange soft bindings,
And I know your weather now
While outside April whitens.

translation by Roland Flint and Ivanka Koviloska-Poposka

Sailor's Song

I left along the distant roads, my apple tree, and now you bloom alone,
my heart is my helmsman, blind yet seeking blue bays,
if I hear the wind in the evening, I forebode your ruin . . .
Has someone's hunger pulled you out by the roots
as I roamed alone?

When the blackbird whistles shrilly three times at dawn,
do not wait for the sun. Listen, I am still digging roads,
on a mast I carry a black flag from tavern to tavern
and hide the pain under my skull.
Oh does the blue lightning bring you a blue downfall,
and do the rains lash you?

I have no more strength to come calm and tall
and to lean my forehead against the sleepy water,
from the blows to rest my hands on the rye until dawn,
and then to go nowhere . . .
My apple tree, the autumn is already here, there is no shore to sail to.
And so I dream of a secluded, small, and deserted harbor.

translation by Vasa D. Mihailovich

SLAVKO JANEVSKI

Silence

When poppies pull themselves up from their roots
and start out
one after the other
toward the sunset
don't follow them.

There are no more weddings
and autumn stands at each step
ridiculous, white and bare.

When the poppies leave devastation behind
close the rain up inside you.
Let it ring in the gutter of your veins
beneath a familiar ceiling.

And be quiet.

When the wind beats against your window
with three thin cries
and the weeping of a half-grown crane
still be quiet.
Poppies hate speaking.

translation by Herbert Kuhner, Howard Erskine-Hill, and Bogomil Gjuzel

ACO ŠOPOV

There's a Blood Down There

There's a heavy blood down there
beating all the way up from the ancient world.
It thickens and dulls the mist on this sharp ridge.
It lies like a scar in a wound.
There's a heavy blood down there. There's blood.
There's a dark blood down there, thick as pitch,
with thirst of a dragon unslaked.
There's an old blood naked and black.
It waits and burrows like a mole.
From door to door it tunnels deep beneath us
as precise and as certain as death.
It throbs into all the empty spaces.
There's a heavy blood down there drumming its code,
"follow, follow, this way, don't go out of range."
There's an awful blood down there, a terrible awe,
There's this heavy blood down there
beating all the way up from the ancient world.

imitation by Roderick Jellema from a translation by Graham W. Reid

In Every Town

In every town there is a man,
and a thirsty but quite tame river;
everyone's weariness will become an olive tree on its shore,
all the smiles will find faithful eyes,
but he will wait, he will wait.

In every town there is a man
with arms like a rainwater tub
for the rain of your autumn,
which will begin gently, but will gush out like a wild river,
until everyone's weariness becomes an olive tree on its shore,

21

until the smiles find the faithful eyes—
but he will wait, he will wait.

Should I go and find my own bed
or give it to some blind traveler
who has not been cured of distrust?
Should I go, and become an olive tree on the shore,
Or hunger after impossibilities?

translation by Milne Holton and Graham W. Reid

Love of Fire

Grave limestone dissolves, seeps to our faces.
Fire startles beneath it like a bird.
Fire flutters its wings from within our time cage.
When a black seed ripens from midnight sun,
Fire is stealing eternal heat from itself
To give some love to its own shooting pain.

Shine, you craved midnight light, shine!
It is here came Prometheus, wounded and alone
Like a dark man-eater, like this hungry earth,
Brought the fire and fell burned.
A stone called fool's gold, that song dissolves.
Longer, the road to man is longer than a life.
The fire is stealing eternal heat from itself
To give some love to its own shooting pain.

Hush, keep silent, keep silent in a young pinewood
Fire and burning, fire and burning.

imitation by Roderick Jellema from a translation by Graham W. Reid

ACO ŠOPOV

The Wind Carries Beautiful Weather

The wind carries beautiful weather.
It raves within us, then resounds.
It carries beautiful weather.

All that's lovely is bright but changes,
and grief remains.
Sometimes grief stretches inside us,
lies down in our eyes
and thickens the layers
that dim the lights we watch.
Then an aching of awe
blows cold and lost, unknown inside us,
haunting us deep.

But then again grief plays light
as breeze in a trembling poplar,
light as a net of mist on the river
that we watch thoughtless and mute.
In those moments all things legend themselves
and we say: how impossibly bright it all is.

The wind raves within us, then resounds.
The wind carries beautiful weather.

imitation by Roderick Jellema from a translation by Ivanka Koviloska-Poposka

Lake

Beat with waves, wheel down, slap the sand,
let clapper of light and your bell of wind ring.
Lake, you swell, and your unquenched tolling
quenches into the shore which is caving in.

23

ACO ŠOPOV

You'll be here when I'm stuck behind some hill without you;
there you'll open fresh inside me like a clam,
like a valley you'll lie down in my eyes,
a pain I cannot see.

Sometimes you won't seem real for days and days.
Often I will think of you as only
fire which is secretly consumed,
someone's heart or someone's blood on fire.

You're a threat when you rise, a shout that glitters;
of all that driftstuff digging in before you
only shadows stay, and sand on the shore
that drinks you into its thirst.

When I'm lost with maps out in that wasteland,
that dumb plain scabbed with black skin
which hears not water but grating springs,
the clatter of two heavy words,

you rise and rinse the crumbling land's end.
You drown in your beauty, suck it far down from the tolling.
Water will know, water will dream everything.
Beat with waves, wheel over, lake; beat, beat.

imitation by Roderick Jellema from a translation by Graham W. Reid

August

I lie down tonight while dying August
sings ashy petals that shoot clean through its terror.
My forehead is loam for a vine of stars
that swells with golden grapes, and ripens.

I lie here in August, my skull knotted to earth.
Will they hold out, can they stop me,
those lines of attacking troops of plant and seed,
of grass, root, and fern?

ACO ŠOPOV

Lie and wait here. Lie still as a stick.
Let the night drink you, let the wind lash,
the fishermen down in your eyes weave gossamer nets,
deep in your waiting there sleeps a golden fish.
I stay awake to feel this August, all the changes.
The high golden grapes like eyeballs are silvering out.
Beneath us the dark sun drifts to its midnight zenith.
Still I lie, tangled and held by grass and fern.

imitation by Roderick Jellema from a translation by Graham W. Reid

Grozomor

Here all things are born of themselves and die out.
A stupendous rock. A scab. Confused and impotent speech.
Spring is its mother and stepmother, wily and mean.
Ashes of dreams, dreams of ashes. Grozomor.

Droughts drink it, black showers drain it.
Layer on layer pile day and night.
Solidified shadows of lust and wild flesh
line up like vertebrae through its crust.

Here hurricanes howl and whirl monstrous shadows.
Here is original sin: crime, judgment, damnation.
Here man and beast sleep in the same hole in a tree,
and a child risks its first unsure step.

Wheat sprouts in the storm from deep, bitter roots,
grows dry and sweet, hot as flames. O my song,

A Macedonian and Serbian word which would lose its force if translated, *grozomor* is an adjective for which the nearest English equivalents, "awful," "horrible," or "monstrous," are not nearly strong enough. Šopov here refers not only to the outrages of the recent war but to all the outrages visited upon the Macedonian people throughout their painful history. ED.

if some hungry and weary pilgrim should reach you,
take him in, and make him your equal in fire.

Rose in the throat, nightshade on the lips,
wild itching of blood which wars with itself,
a land of deadly and exquisite poisons,
the stone tumbles into the flames. Burns. Burns. And burns.

Here all things are born of themselves and die out.
A stupendous rock. A scab. Confused and impotent speech.
Spring is its mother, deceitful stepmother.
Ashes of dreams, dreams of ashes. Grozomor.

translation by Elisavietta Ritchie and Eugene Prostov

Reader of Ashes

Burn out, song, in the fire you have struck.
Your flint has split the word and burned it to ashes.
Reader of ashes, do you see in the ashes the fable
which rises from deep in that gray?
Song, I broke you off from the birdbeak aflight in my blood,
from the red sky of my fired veins, strung
from pylons charged at opposite poles.
I broke you off from red and black anger of icons,
from the thunder in the warrior's stone-tipped spear,
from dreams of men who are taller than their dreams
and rise again from their ashes.
It has split the world in two, its sides clash
in a winless war, knife against knife.
Who loses? Who wins? Who will make sense
of the sunrise of wounds?
Burn out, song, in the fire you have struck.

imitation by Roderick Jellema from a translation by Graham W. Reid

ACO ŠOPOV

Birth of the Word

Ankle over ankle.[1]
Stone over stone.
Stony wood.
Stone cold.
Ankle over ankle.
Stone over stone,
both of us from stone.
The night is soot black.
The word divides from the darkness.
Blue coal burns in the bowels.
Oh, you that exist why don't you exist?
You rock the sky.
You turn the earth.
Oh, you that exist why don't you exist?
The earth groans under stone pavements.
It comes drunk from its deaths,
the word that smashes all the temples.
Ankle over ankle.
Stone over stone,
I dig my grave with damnation.
Open me,
you damnation,
you fortress of stone,
to burn away in the coal of the word,
to melt.

translation by Biljana Dimovska

This and the next two poems are taken from a cycle of twelve poems collected under the general title of *Prayers for My Body*. The cycle begins with "Birth of the Word"; the second poem, "Prayer for a Simple Word, Not Yet Discovered," is also the first prayer. The set continues through ten, and then a "Last" prayer. ED.

1. *Gluźd,* here translated as "ankle" (after Serbo-Croatian *Gleźanj*), can also mean "a knot in wood." It is the awareness of this double meaning which generates the poem. ED.

27

Prayer for a Simple Word, Not Yet Discovered

My whole being begs you:
Discover a word that resembles a simple tree
and the palms of the hand, petrified and primevially naked,
that is like the innocence of each first prayer.
My being begs you for such a word.

My whole being begs you:
Discover a word from which—as soon as uttered with a cry—
unconsciously the blood begins to ache,
blood that seeks a channel to flow.
My being begs you for such a word.

Discover a word so true
it resembles those peaceful prisoners
and that wind, that spring wind
that wakes the deer in our eyes.
Discover such a true word.

Discover a word about birth, about wailing,
discover a word so true. And this temple,
enveloped in its antiquity and huge from waiting,
will open obediently, all by itself.
Discover a word about birth, about wailing.

translation by Vasa D. Mihailovich

Second Prayer for My Body

This body, a bridge between two shores,
Lives in the dawns of your desires,
Unaltered tomorrow except for the scars
Of two more wounds it suffered today,
Outstretched like a bridge between two shores.

28

ACO ŠOPOV

Outstretched like a bridge, this body awaits
The carefree fellow who will rouse him again . . .
Flow under this body, O river constrained,
May the rush of feelings surge through the arches
Stretched like a bridge where this body lies waiting.

As a bridge awaits the water's embrace,
Its forgotten image revealed in the depth,
By imagined desires awakened and changed,
This body will stand like a lighthouse tower
That now as a bridge awaits the water's embrace.

translation by Daniel Hoffman

A Toast

I raise this glass to you—
to everyone, to whatever you want,
to you, to good luck, I tell them,
but—well—my hand is empty.

translation by Milne Holton and Lena Ognenova

II

The Middle Generation

SRBO IVANOVSKI

Every Night

Every night, I take you away
from the ordinary things:
away from the mirror,
the needles,
the broken windows,
the same old room
with the same old chairs.
I take you so far away,
so far away,
that I leave you on grass, and you sink
to rise up freshened,
pearled with dew,
with fresh dew.
You stand there as if cut in marble,
but warm—
warm like the lake's murmur.
Lie on the grass
and watch the disturbing snakes;
silently they will leave us,
silently return at dusk;
Lie down and watch, stretching
from us to its end,
the green of the valley.

translation by Milne Holton

White Stone

Out of strange dreams I build strange graves;
each white stone is the fruit of a dead dream.
I wear the cold stones you gave me on each finger
and the great winter settles inside us.

33

The bare feet and the dust are born somewhere far away,
but the dreams will descend even from the white wall.
After all, did we not invent the sky
so that we might strive for something?
But for death we have only white stone.

We are restless between the two green mornings.
The word is that terrible caterpillar
who consumes us when the fruit is gone.
Now I must search for my own white stone.

translation by Myra Sklarew and Lena Ognenova

Minaret

. . . the landscape of the past. A dream
pointed toward the stars. A silver fish
imprisoned in blue. A cold smile
of the years. Written in the steep rock.

The day like the sun's flame on the forehead
falls to the street. A constellation of sounds.
Trifles bought for a song. A fountain
of earth and stone kindled at dusk,

and the dream is burned down; poured out to the stars.
That time calls. So I say, tell me
about your uneasiness. I say. I whisper. I shout.
It answers with mute signs.

imitation by Myra Sklarew

Rest

When the warrior took off his armor,
he knew how the south wind
reached even the seed of the fruit.

It was a day when each of us
became distant, remote.
Even her motion was haunted.

Yet the air was charmed
by the touch of her shoulder
on the bee's way.

The bush has turned into smoke,
on fire
with the young green fruit.

We were one
with the moss of the fortress,
shadows and the ghosts of shadows.

translation by Myra Sklarew

Word

I closed you up in stone
as in a jewel box,
in the bottom of stone,
in a place as solitary as Van Gogh's room;
I closed you in silence, in your own silence.
Yet here you are again,
like a cold spring,
like a drop fresh in the grass.

I gave you to the fire—
did you know of my crime?
He only did it
who had borne fire from song to song.

I made a sword of you,
a red sword with a white blade;
are you now that sweet pain
that stops my breath when I smile?

translation by Milne Holton and Graham W. Reid

Ohrid Troubadours

The island is there—the longing
for time, unreality, dreams, for an elusive star.
It sprouts inside us first,
but it flowers only on the edge of the abyss.

The moment is there—the castle
without walls or gates, vain fortress of a word,
the green fountain where the rainbow grows
to offer dreams of sleeplessness.

The shore is there—razed by thirst and flame,
and a bird's cry, a cry turned to stone.
Set out softly; the foam still sleeps,
and the castle without walls, or door, or dream, or moment.

translation by Milne Holton and Lena Ognenova

Flight

This mountain continues to invent new snows.
When will it make time for the tired summer
which lies along the slope chained in poppies?

SRBO IVANOVSKI

Before the ripe fruits came, I came running.
Fate of the ridges, where should I plant
my flight?
For a handful of silence I laid rugs on the road.
Mother, when I began crying,
you will know me as a newborn.
Spellbound by the sun,
the fortress of my words crumbles.
How may I forget my ruins?

imitation by Nancy Marks from a translation by B. Kunovska

Calling the Lightning

Storm
I call to the lightning
and its signals of black expeditions.
I want the earth, that tense
song in huddled folds on my doorstep,
I want the earth to shake loose
the restless horses
whose dry muzzles want water,
whose wet wombs are on fire.
The earth is a dry mouth
and green shoots from twigs.
I want the sky to split.
That white, torn cry
of the lightning shouts me down.

Song
The song gets lost in a sleep
or crumbles
in the strange storm
or in the moment of hush
still glanced with knives of lightning.

37

It sings in the day that flies
it rains on our lonely island
or the fat summer wind that brings rain
that laves its mane of yellow leaves in the soft dust.

The song and I are still
when the lightnings call each other.

Fear

The mountain is shivering
and the quiet blanket of fog cannot help,
but the doe will not see herself
in the red river of lightning.
Fear has eyes that are bigger
even than death.

imitation by Roderick Jellema from a translation by B. Kunovska

The City on My Palms

I built a city on my palms
green-fenced it with goodness
to keep out the wolves and foxes.
Built a city without tenants
a city with all its smiles facing the sun
a city with many girls and boys in love
who part late in the evening.

My neighbor will never set foot in it
nor the lady at the end of the street.
A girl quieter than a shadow will live there
who has only one dream: to be a river
and to rock the stars at night
and the white clouds during the day.

translation by Vasa D. Mihailovich

ANTÉ POPOVSKI

Sunflowers

Suddenly to the plain in the darkness came April
In a hot breath,
And through the summer the earth was dark and our saints sang darkly
Of our past tumbling darkly toward us bearing disaster.

Now darkness circles our forts, kindles the times,
Fireless.
We watch as the wind scatters our hope's ash.

What is it there in the dust moistens the sunflower?
The flower takes to its roots, drop by drop, like a child,
The milk of bitterness.
Wounds in its angel head see the black and gold.
A tree trunk cracks in the sun; nothing is spared
The vagabond in its shadow seeking the darkness-love.

The blood shrieks.
The bone decomposes.
Everything under the sun rings out
The stars' devastation.
                              Must we persist
On our island of futures?

Oh, Macedonia,
In front of your map we stand singing our matins.
The sunflowers tremble
                              in the plain's old misery,
                              in the darkness.

an abbreviated rendering by Reed Whittemore after a translation by Graham W. Reid

ANTÉ POPOVSKI

From *Macedonia*

Here a plain land of two-faced stone and sun
Where children still unable to walk dig up skulls
in the gardens.

Here a plain land of cobwebs and water
Where freedom wisely records the villagers' names
In place of ikons in the churches,
And where summer, like destiny,
Lasts to the last rebel.

Here a plain land of weary breathing and silence
Through which time passes and returns once more
To share with it the false permanence.

Yes, it is here, a plain land of convulsion and expectation
That taught even the stars to whisper in Macedonian
And no one knows it.

. . . .

For the wolves' cry and the terror of the heavens was my land made
Without cypresses or rainbows,
To the last drop, three days before it appeared above my head
The graveyards drained the cloud
And a knife's black shadow instead of a cross is cast on the stone that
 covers you
For all time.
For nothing else befits this wild growth, those dark mountains,
Except to wait for what is yet to come.

translation by Graham W. Reid

ANTÉ POPOVSKI

Vineyard

You have deserted me.
You have left me out on the mountain under the sky.
At noon I feed from the sun; I nightly caress rock.

In October,
When my leaves are brown and the hands that cared for me wither,
The wind then and the bareness will make an end of me.

Why do you care not?
Why do you not anticipate your own end
When my leaves must assume your paternity and you sleep?

You have deserted me.
You have left me out on the mountain under the sky
To feed from the sun.

rendering by Reed Whittemore after a translation by Graham W. Reid

Woman

When we decided to move to another country
in the morning came a voice:

Woman
who stayed in the north,
as motionless as a scar, a skeleton,

where are you? Are you singing
somewhere, leaning against some wall?
Why not here to heal the wound
you left in my soul?

ANTÉ POPOVSKI

Bitter woman,
are you looking at this burnt-out sun
as it moves from hill to hill, from south to south?

Do you see me charred,
burned alive in the past?

translation by Milne Holton and Graham W. Reid

From *Samuel*

There was nothing left for man:
The lava rose over the horror,
Overflowing the gulfs,
Leveling the chasms.
The rivers were effaced
By the rock,
          Hard, black rock.

The moon no longer set
Over the axis of the plains.
Grain was no longer seen on the threshing floors.

Tsar Samuel (or Samuil) was the last fully autonomous ruler of the short-lived but vital Macedonian empire, which achieved independence from the Bulgarians in A.D. 969 and survived until 1018. Under Samuel (976–1014) Ohrid became a patriarchate and reached its cultural apogee; Samuel built a fortress there overlooking the lake, and its ruins still stand; they are frequently mentioned in the contemporary poetry.

Samuel expanded his empire as far north as the environs of Zadar on the Adriatic and had ambitions for hegemony over all the Balkans; he struggled with the Greeks, and his armies posed a serious threat to Basil II's Byzantium. Basil

ANTÉ POPOVSKI

The trees bore rock instead of fruit,
And the peasants took it in their hands like bread.
And instead of children, the pregnant women
brought forth rock.
             Hard, black rock.

The wild animals howled through the forests.
The last she-wolf died on a dry outcropping.
It will no longer give birth to wolves.

And the wide winds, driven mad,
Blew enormous ashes,
And heaped them one upon the other,
And higher than centuries, pushed the rock.
The bare rock, the black rock.

Nothing, nothing left for man.
It rose up over the horror,
And the gulfs overflowed,
And the chasms leveled,
And the rivers effaced
By the rock,
The bare rock, the black rock.

translation by John Woodbridge and Carolyn Kizer

---

finally defeated Samuel's armies at Belasica in 1014, and, according to tradition, Basil undertook to rid himself of Samuel's threat forever by blinding every man of the defeated army, some fifteen thousand men strong. Every hundredth man was left one eye to lead his fellows home. When Samuel met them at Prilep on their return, he was so horrified that he suffered a heart attack and died two days later.

Samuel's empire was thus destroyed, and the Byzantines conquered Macedonia in 1018. So today Macedonians regard Samuel's defeat at Belasica as the beginning of nearly a thousand years of subjugation and oppression of their people.

This selection is from part one of Popovski's five-part dramatic poem. ED.

CANÉ ANDREEVSKI

White Song by the Lake

O you white bells,
White bells with a song of white,
Strike on this shore.

O you white bells,
Sound white, white.

Unhinge the black gates,
Leap across black thresholds
Enter the black courtyards.

O you white bells,
Enter the black courtyards
And be white bells,
White bells in a throat of white.

translation by Graham W. Reid

Framed Place

When you find this place,
when you find it again,
you can frame it,
you can put it under glass.

Let the frame be dark
since the place is bright.

Hang it on the wall
beside the big clock
that cuts time
into confetti.

Let it fly beside it;
the frame will stay dark
and the place bright.

translation by Herbert Kuhner and Duško Tomovski

CANÉ ANDREEVSKI

Celebration

Let the celebration begin!
Let our names swing
instead of lanterns.
Reach out
and shake hands with the sea.
Everyone should discover for himself
the threads which connect him
with the silver of the sea,
with the gull's wing,
with the island's cove,
with the furrow that a ship cuts.

Close your eyes for a moment
and open them to the world
cleansed of the last poisonous tear.

Embellish yourself with an enchanted flower
for you have only one chance
to toast with the glasses
filled with forgetfulness and forgiveness.

Music!
Let the celebration begin!
Serenity dances on the stage of the sea.

The visible edge of the sea
does not signify the end of the celebration.

translation by Herbert Kuhner and Duško Tomovski

CANÉ ANDREEVSKI

You and I
For Zlatko

You hide behind every new word;
how difficult it will be to find each other!

Tame the words.
Let them be silent so that you can be with me.

translation by Herbert Kuhner and Duško Tomovski

GANÉ TODOROVSKI

The Evening Ruffled by Wind

The afternoon is poor in colors.
The grayness—
that ugly, confining decor.
Wrapped in stupid uniformity
the street stretches sadly,
and you sense, so to speak,
that familiar
that awful emptiness
that so often settles on the city.
And it is just fine that it came tonight,
this crazed,
this exuberant
wind born for pranks:
may its nonexistent hands blossom
to find peace and rest,
this vagabond that can
brighten our foreheads,
rub our eyes,
redden our cheeks,
so that we yearn and immerse
childishly
into all ruffles of this world.
For it is delightful indeed
to tousle someone's curls
just as it is to pass from an empty afternoon
into the evening ruffled by wind.

translation by Vasa D. Mihailovich

47

GANÉ TODOROVSKI

Welcome

At that time a mother heard her son's voice, she called, "My son!"
Her son came to her at the same instant as freedom. From a memoir

Weariness is a track in the mind of nonsleepers;
waiting fills it with unease;
but the eye and the ear are thresholds of hope,
hidden away
from suspicion, that silent monster.

Twilight feels like a lever
which one must lift alone for a long time;

unease in the heart is a guest,
but the night is an endless waste of silence.

No. The night can be a bridge
on which a measured step will cross,
and with it long held hope,
to meet the brightness in the gray, naked day,
to meet the joy we anticipate

and him amidst them.

translation by Milne Holton and Vlado Cvetkovski

Seven Returns to a Trembling Aspen Tree

1
Green eyelashes with no sleep.
Green, dumb, fluttering.
a meadow beauty,
hungry for sleep.

2
Her body is green butterflies
ravaged in an upward flow.

48

3

Dying for rest, restless
she wastes time trembling upright,
peeping into the clouds,
following the road,
longing for the gypsies.

She is chilled
even in the sweat of no wind in midsummer.

4

Is it lack of sleep or terror that shakes her?
Terrible sin? Barrenness?
Or is she merely daydreaming?

5

Had she been my godchild,
I would have named her the Restless One.
Sleepless, restless, barren, upstreaming in the meadow.
Had I been an evening harbinger,
I would have plucked that trembling,
her gesture of terrible loneliness.

6

She herself will tell you how much she is startled.
Her constant trembling: at daybreak! at noon! at sunset!

7

She envies the birds
who nest in her lap:
the sleep, the children,
the peace.

The sleepless one. The barren one. Green, restless one.

translation by Edward Gold and Vlado Cvetkovski

A White Butterfly I Called My Love

White butterfly of my dark dreams,
shake spring from your wings; then go—
I know the wind will blow you beyond return,
and the roads will lead me to weariness,
to black nights, not azure mornings.

Child of April, play your fine game of lies
as in the child's story when the dead awake,
weave with your words the webs of silver spiders,
as in a winter midnight when we are enchanted
by unannounced dreams or insane foreshadowings.

. . . Once there was a strange boy,
who wondered, with two minds and three hundred wishes,
whether to gather the things without feeling
or to embrace what he had been promised
in the ungrasped half-truths of dream . . .

But the vagueness is both the good and the evil.
How do we know what is the cleverest choice in this world?
Our small wishes are sometimes so funny;
they stand us upright, ugly thirsty creatures,
between the holy and the cursed, reaching for the forbidden.

But there is a fine for hesitation;
for every story must have its end;
open the door a bit, leave us a way out,
. . . he was destined, they say, to wander and to suffer,
the boy of the story, the one born in May . . .

White butterfly, visitor to my dark dreams,
Fly away somewhere—to nowhere, if you've been already—
The curse is bitter for those forgiven
the sin not sinned, the crime not committed.
The curse is for those who have touched your wings.

translation by Milne Holton and Vlado Cvetkovski

GANÉ TODOROVSKI

A Quiet Step
For Jončé Naumov

1

Over the gray and grooved contours of the suburb
twilight pours a somber dust
and like a harbinger of the coming night
sets out the effects of evening.

We feel on us the weight of the cool scent of darkness.

I think he thought: night is a pitiless little square
which closes in all lonely people;
and he set out toward the threshold of that night,
he set out in the clamorous twilight, sunk deep into himself.

I believe: the well of the night attracts the lonely ones,
making them a harbor hidden from the eyes of the world.
Often the sad prayers we send up at dawn were whispered in him.
Often he felt no kinship with mankind.

I think he thought: the night is a peaceful clearing
from which the weary seek a little rest.

2

The next morning we found him in the hospital chapel,
alone again, on a concrete slab,
again a prisoner of that loneliness he had expected, in a flash,
to leave behind.
His eyes were open and clear,
like the sky after the rain on a May night,
and they looked like a greeting, warm and innocent.
For us, again, we wanted to find the answer that led
to that flight.
As though his eyes were a fissure through which
we could discern the reason
for the act which that October night had hidden from us.
Perhaps, like Whitman, we could call it "ruin,"

this body that the mortuary chapel now
throws before our uncertain feet,
this frail, beautiful form
which so short a time ago we knew as a student
and for whom the obituaries announced:
Died in an accident.

3

Nobody knew why he'd fled from the living,
stretching his body out along the rails, not far from town.
He went out mute as the steel that wrapped him in its cold arms,
hoping, perhaps, never to be destroyed by loneliness.

Today he is a memory among the souvenirs of his friends,
he's an epitaph on a stone that will never speak
of the mute despair of that ending,
of that quiet step accomplished
in the night of October 8.

4

Sometimes, when I turn to Sandburg
I stop, not without reason, at that verse where the old man says:

> *And death is a quiet step*
> *into a sweet clean midnight.*[1]

translation by Heddy Reid

A Night Without Punctuation

Toward the shore we sail
We,
lonesome travelers . . .

---

1. The line is from Carl Sandburg's "The Man with the Broken Fingers," a poem about the torture of a Norwegian partizan by the Germans, dated August 23, 1942. ED.

GANÉ TODOROVSKI

It hurts, the flared-up fatigue!
If we could only find the way
to be born again
again
in the naked mornings.

And bare thoughts
tremble;
restlessness scratches
the skin of the night.
In the boat of hope
we sail
O dawn,
toward you,
cast down upon our eyelids,
which have grown heavy.

And no one has the strength,
even an ounce of strength
to make even a comma!

But we hate the full stops.

translation by Vasa D. Mihailovich

In the Night

In the night scraped by anxieties
silence is a bed for the weary
for those whose anxiety was buried

In the night perforated by thoughts
tedium is an unending climb
up a path lit by hope

In the night filled with hope
whatever is sheltered in a corner of the brain
is cramped by doubt

53

GANÉ TODOROVSKI

In the night worn by doubt
thoughts are a quiet field
that draws us into its vastness

In the night worn by tedium
premonition is a prisoner in the self
where the only ornament is a sigh

imitation by Milne Holton from a translation by Herbert Kuhner and Duško
Tomovski

Late Spring Near Nerezi

Very often, as soon as the dawn shows,
we make this ascent.
With its soft hillocks, the slope lures upward
our tired steps: uneven and hospitable verdure.

As far as one sees, lovely fields of wheat
and the tangled carpet of vineyards, vineyards, vineyards.
By the side of the serpentine road, the huge elms.
On the road, our quick tread.

We happen on the hurrying little brook,
the jester of Sultan Sui,
and are greeted by the men of Saint Petka
going down into the village with their heavy cares
and a little bit of yoghurt to sell.

An hour and a half on the way, and here we are
in this quiet corner we love.

On the side of Mt. Vodno, just above Skopje, stands the monastery of St.
Panteleimon, in the village of Nerezi. The ancient monastery is now a resort. St.
Petka (an active monastery) and Sultan Sui (a spring) are places one encounters in
making the climb up to Nerezi and St. Panteleimon. ED.

GANÉ TODOROVSKI

The women are spreading wool coverlets
beneath the chestnut trees, already at their gossip.
Our glance drifts toward the lowlands,
toward the lowlands, the fields
where the heat is grilling Skopje.

translation by Heddy Reid

Sketch for the First Letter to Ema Germova

Born for awakening on my love-day—
the first one and the last one. I call you mine.
All the day long I will want you, until that day,
and I count days until I can count no more.

Je t'aime, ya lyublyu tebya, ich liebe dich,
how else should I say it?
How confused is this unfinished line
before a strange woman, before her beloved silence.

I suffer a word, I speak suffering,
I get not over pain, I burn not out,
and one day I'm afraid I'll be ruined
by fine women or bad wine.

Little time is left for me to be young in;
my poem guards me like a faithful dog
from all the griefs we grieved,
from all the joys we joyed,
we, who won and are defeated.

Miser words, fond traitors,
you tell her.
For you we avoided every whirlpool and rock
in the heart of the man you should hold,
in the fondness of your unrest.

imitation by Milne Holton from a translation by Graham W. Reid

GANÉ TODOROVSKI

Sonatina

And now there is only peace—
dreamed of, desired peace,
the loneliness, the freshness.

A butterfly flutters solemnly,
an ash-colored butterfly,
across a windy field.

It is so quiet here,
mysterious, quiet,
a good place for sadness.

The enchanted silence takes us,
it seizes the deadly minutes—
the silence, the silence.

translation by Milne Holton, Herbert Kuhner, and Duško Tomovski

MATEJA MATEVSKI

The Tree in the Valley

1

A small tree,
lonely and ugly curves,
black, withered black, in the valley,

two branches, a trunk, and a silence.
It looks like a man who suffered;
it is hammered and buried in the soil.

It does not remember many days,
or snow or rain or winds or grass;
birds do not nest in it.

It stands there, as bare as a cross,
like a man hammered into the ground,
like a corpse grinning at you.

A sandy mouth and a stone trunk.

2

This tree, dry and alone,
has eyes like the south winds,
that gaze beyond the sunsets,

but the winds don't come here;
God forgot this valley
in the chilly dark.

The waters and the dark rocks crumble,
the wild beasts cry,
they gnaw at the bark.

And yet it stands, poised for flight,
the dreaming winds give it food,
it gazes beyond the sunsets,

and sunset is not sunset here.

57

3

Where there's no sun there's no dawn, no sunset
nor the darkness before which one weeps
nor space nor time nor loneliness;

Everything's deaf; there's nothing.
Yet the tree grows. Slowly.
Not knowing.

Here only the earth says softly

that something happens,
And that there's a slender spring in it
which knows everything.

translation by Milne Holton and Graham W. Reid

Bells

Ringing somewhere: somewhere far
The sounds are wind waves
In the fugitive grass.

Ringing somewhere: sharp, steady, soft;
All else is deaf; only the beat
Bounds on the wrought rim.

Ringing somewhere: hurl me in air;
Fly through the rung cage,
deafly and helplessly.

Ringing somewhere: like a child I ring, sing,
Everything's locked, I sound spellbound,
Hang on the sound.

Ringing somewhere: strike me, brave, tamed,
Time, strike my memory,
Rude and so greedy.

Ringing somewhere: long hence but now.
Everything aches. Sky, let me down
With the grass. I know sound.

*imitation by Milne Holton from a translation by Graham W. Reid, Biljana
Dimovska, and Katica Todorovska*

From *Equinox*

This is an hour of calm, a quiet hour,
an idyll of days and nights like a folding of hands
The sky soft on the stretched body of the plain
Now is the hour when nothing happens
as if the world didn't breathe as if the rain didn't pour
a dream enclosed in the dark of a hazelnut
a stone forgotten under the body of a hill
Now is the instant when wheat is harvested
when the chimney does not smoke nor the road resound
Man lies beneath the body of the sun
distilled into nothing by its shadows
This is the total moment: the balance of black and white

translation by Carolyn Kizer and Graham W. Reid

Rains

1. Fear

Now come the sluggish, come the exhausted horses of space
the far and foreboding murmur of the forgotten tongue.
Clip-clopping unceasingly, alone before the closed windows,
muffled clip-clopping, blunted legs without horseshoes,
on you, earth, slippery, loamy, calm earth,
clip-clopping darkly mingled.

Where before this mass, before this cotton
horizon without outline,
before this dark flesh of earth and night,
flesh both deeply mixed and dense,
a flood upon the eyes, and upon the spaces death?

Where, O where, you and I, you, sea, noisy and endless,
you monotone field, horizontally tired,
craving the upright brightness of the winds?
Where, O where,
you compact dough of rain and earth,
O man, me,
stone in the hands and in the eyes, mud?

2. The Song
Where, where do you come from, known and unforgettable
song, your child naive and desperate,
you arrow of grass and bird from the mud,
dried and endless path through the rain,
silvery path, winding like a snake,
where are you leading me?

Always foreboding in the waters and darkness,
you sweet mane, sweet and rugged,
not passively bold,
flesh, muscular, of earth and night,
sharp mane, restless sabre of seeing
on the silvery path of space
like radiant lightning.

And take me away, take me away, childhood,
take me away, song, eternal, unforgettable age,
you greatest illusion without metaphor,
you clumsily opened window, dangerous and deep,
opened to all the colors of eternity.
Take me away through the rain,
then bring me back, kind path, to this small haven,
to this soft nest of dreams.

3. Horses

Now come the sluggish, come the exhausted horses of space
(pale rains, pathless and mute)
before the palms of my hands on the window.

Feed, I say, feed yourselves, horses! sweating
and wet from the warm vapor filtering
from the loins of the night.

Playfully whinny, make me cry out for joy,
spring, bird with forgotten wings,
goat-leg dancer, tired and exhausted mare,
through my window spring
together and back again
and ever without ceasing
under the shadowy brightness of space.

translation by Howard Erskine-Hill and Bogomil Gjuzel

Rain-Horses

See, they stumble, they splash like horses asleep
through weary space, these pale and dumb rains,
plowing this sea of window glass under my hands.

Rain, for food I think you could graze on horses,
sweating a wet warm steam
that breathes through parted lips of the night.

Twang into whinny the cords in my throat!
Spring! you bird with forgotten wings,

Although we have not ordinarily included alternate translations of single
poems, Roderick Jellema's version of the third part of Matevski's "Rains" seemed
worthy of inclusion here, not only for its distinction as a separate poem, but for
the opportunity to compare this reversion with the more literal translation by
Gjuzel and Erskine-Hill. ED.

goat-legged dancer, loping and tattered mare,
through my window spring
converge and blow back
in waves, time out of mind
through these dappled, dark-and-bright fields of space.

imitation by Roderick Jellema from the preceding translation

A Dark Circlet of Fogs

Into my eyes on a beautiful day
You brought darkness and blinded me
But I am not a nest for sorrows
Nor a wind to think you out into nothingness

In me there is a flower of fading color
That cannot touch the petals of the sun
It doesn't know how to burst open
Before that yellow light
Unaware of the resistance
Of the dark soil of gloom

Thus calmly poised before the concentric wisps
Of fog which surround me I sow
for one only innumerable question marks in the wind and the darkness
consumed now by the slow centipede of silence

I've known and understood all autumn fogs
Only you escape me and remain dark
Stretched out at my feet like the earth before ploughing
But how can I know if sage or tumbleweed
Will flower in the spring

And this thought without the passion of a ploughman before sowing
makes me arise from you fog who fill me with gloom
For I would know who you are and why I bow down before you

as to an ancient altar of the ages
Where I was diminished to ashes a thousand times
Sweetly and for nothing

You know how to send me your beautiful smile
But how shall I understand it how clutch it in my hands
How vanquish your silence
I need the word with which I can say
What there is in this body
Which like a fog surrounds and invades me

But when I open my eyes and everything's gone
The sky clears the fog suspends
Last necklaces from the throats of trees
And in the street I am blind and deceived
Naked as I was born and deaf as the dead

I am the tree in a noose of fog

translation by Daniel Hoffman

Holiday Romance

Morning: Travel

The sun has thrown torches into our rooms;
they singe the walls, they swallow the windows, they set us on edge,
on this holiday morning full of shouts,
this morning full of nothing
but thoughts of a blue and silent sky,
of green waters washing a dry shore,
which the sun has brought us.

Into our bags and backpacks
go our small desires;
with thin songs and leftover laughter
we will fill our field of vision—

with sky and birds and grass and water
which don't know the smoky taste
of this and all our summer mornings.

Everything is so quiet and beautiful and good;
you will be like a bird, the grass, a waterfall
foaming with colors to wash your eyes.
With a damp cloth it will wash your dream of memory,
it will fill your breast with greenness,
it will make you a little more human.

Noon: In the Ring
How soft is the sun's zenith
        at noon
by the hazels flowing in mirrors
        on the river,
but down in the depths of the earth
        another fire burns
to change us into dogs, into vultures,
        into people
with no interest in primal peace.

Like a pack of wolves we have slaughtered the lambs
        of the green plants,
we have crushed the ants, the insects,
        with their green blood,
we have tossed the filth of our oaths
        into the river,
we have smeared the sky
        with our shouts,
with our foolish movement
        we have spoiled the shadows;
Tears of green fruit
        hang from the hazels.
For a little more water we have disturbed,
        destroyed,
        dammed up the springs.

MATEJA MATEVSKI

And now we hate one another,
we argue about a seat in the train,
about the ball which fell in the lunch;
    we get excited,
our tongues becomes knives,
our hands hooks.
And then there are no more tears, no more contemptuousness,
    nor more of the walk,
    nothing,
    not even the peace.
Then, with the havoc, the bitterness behind us,
exhausted,
sated,
we go home.

Evening: A Change
The curtains open.
The wind, that old friend of night,
bears the fresh red smell of evening,
spreads weariness and the soothing memory
of walking among the many things
which are between two towns.

Sleep has not yet dropped our heavy eyelids,
a bit of the sky's blue is still in the eyes,
the ear still ruffles with the lullaby of hens
and the cries of the cats in the rubbish
and those people's squabble about punishing their child.

O how good we were today,
far from this dark deadliness,
far from this tin-canned downtown,
deep in the silence of soft grass,
of gentle birds and gentler waters;
we were so good, so fine, so trusting,
on this short day of rest,

65

of respite from the sun's curse
on our city summer.

Our eyelids drop with new desires,
our arms and legs and necks loosen
like flowers reddening with sunset,
we are so good in that sleep filled with memory,
and just at the corners of our lips
we still hold
a torn,
a tiny
trace of a smile.

Is it the bitterness of coming undone silently;
or perhaps just the fine and simple change
that comes with night?

*imitation by Milne Holton and Nancy Marks from a translation by Graham W.
Reid*

Lake

After many years and many dreams
I have come back
to this lake with its fresh water
lost in the lap of the hills.

The diamond of the sun
still pierces
no stone in its depths,
not even the grass,
which hides its throat
under the waves,
nor the bird which bears its prey.

I am an eye, only an eye, of the sun
which moves its ancient water.

Leave me beside this lake,
leave me beside this lake,
beside its bitterness.
Leave me here to die.

translation by Milne Holton and Graham W. Reid

Ballad of Time

I listen to time dying

Beside the falling leaves
and the frost nipping at hands
how far did I get

Time dies in all that is born
and there is always less and less of me
even if by a step

Autumn is rich in dreams
if sometimes sad
in the receding waters
there is no sailing

The rich November fogs
what do the rivers nurse them with
In their shallow waters
how far shall I get

I listen to time dying

From autumn in the cold
one fruit is left
that asks with blue lips
where shall I get to

translation by Vasa D. Mihailovich

III
The New Poets

VLADA UROŠEVIĆ

Another City

There is another city within this city,
which is there when one enters,
which one perceives
first of all
in the guise of a light slowing up
of movement on the square
and the naive resemblance
of the corner of a house
to a shoulder moving slightly
when one glances backward.
A city exists
whose boundaries
merge
like rain and fog
with the cement frontiers of that city
you find on all the maps.
Nevertheless,
at times it suffices
to turn one's head slightly,
and these two boundaries
fit into each other
like shadows into their objects
at noon.
Then we post ourselves
before the jutting decorations of a house
that looks like a startled face,
eyes opened wide
as in old photographs,
and we laugh
as if we were discovering it for the first time.
Then this city becomes a different city,
and I'm not at all sure
that this one you find on the maps.

translation by Elisavietta Ritchie and Eugene Prostov

VLADA UROŠEVIĆ

Workshop

Behind blind walls
indifferent houses
the grass grows
surrounding rusty machines
blunted by the sun.
All around are high fences
and beyond them a town
where people pass, dogs stop
uncomprehending.
Here, between slow movements
and endless talk
people with preoccupied faces
make from old iron
parts for certain machines
whose function
is not completely explained.

translation by Linda Pastan and Graham W. Reid

The Guardian of the Tower

The horsemen rode up from the east. Dust caked
their faces and sheepskin capes.
Heat poured down, and amid the silence and fear
the slow and heavy rain began to fall.

And he, the guardian of the tower, stood alone on the ramparts.
The grasshoppers still cried their sharp dry cries.
One final time the air bore fragrances from the invisible sea.
As never before, the insects droned in his ears.

He came down as they forced the gates. He fought
surrounded. Blood and sweat were intermixed, sweat and blood.

They flung him down among bird droppings and piled weapons
while frightened summer birds circled overhead.

translation by Elisavietta Ritchie and Eugene Prostov

The Freedom of Dreamers

The island they seek is far away,
don't bother to shout.
For them it's simple
to swim against the current.

They toss away their shoes
and seize the golden fleece.
Soaring from the alders
they feed the birds by their beaks.

Chance lifts them high,
they steer through the dark.
Waking is their prison
A dream sets them free.

translation by Linda Pastan and Graham W. Reid

Summer Rain

You can't generalize about summer rain;
here we have a summer rain which knocks
and urges me to announce it somehow,
in an unshackled tongue, with a drummerless drum;

to announce it somehow, with a word all bubbles,
with an incomplete sentence through which,
in the language of mutes, the argument will be expressed
between runnel and gurgle; to proclaim it in a water mill

73

of consonants and water where reason is ground,
in a masticated alphabet, in a lofty useless law
on the descent of noise; to proclaim it any which way
in stunned speech, in a splashing

which is understood. There exists just this rain,
and it's hard to find words which aren't lies.
There exists just this rain which will not consent
to enter a poem unless it also is wet.

translation by Elisavietta Ritchie

An Ancient Landscape

Once again the barren weeds intertwine in the evening waters
of the canal where the reflected sky doubles the image of
the black unfinished bridge. As in a postcard, a woman walks
in the distance with her white parasol; she stands like a guest

in this landscape which pays no attention to her and opens
like a fruit. The horizon becomes a child's sketch pad, the grass
straightens up, while someone introduces there on the hill
some twilight contraptions, nests, and horse-cabs thin

and fragile with age. Lonely people emerge
from their ground-floor apartments, hope for some event hitherto
unknown, and speak in low voices of the woman who is gone.

And the horizon crumbles like an old picture, and where
nut trees grew, now the village merry-go-round is departing,
or else it is the funeral of the double bass.

translation by Elisavietta Ritchie

VLADA UROŠEVIĆ

The City at Sunset

The city suffers from a loss of equilibrium
at sunset: each street leans a bit.
The shadows of tar and glass lie on the squares
and children leapfrog over them.

Gnats in the air: the air teems with gnats.
Fire in the greenhouses. Glassworks are burning.
A taxi flees across the sunshine aimlessly.
The cyclists are but shining meteors.

The sun sets and the city's head aches.
Malarial fever seizes the windows.
The temperature rises again in the freshly hosed park.
The druggist's vials are flashing warnings.

translation by Elisavietta Ritchie

The Sleepers

Living people pass close by them
while they sleep in the parks
amid the rush, between two trains,
their faces open like swamp flowers
strange strangers
persistent in their absences
as void of memory as drowned men
relinquishing their hands
their fingers, which now lie there
like aquatic creatures with transparent bodies
dragged on dry sand,
indifferent, impassive,

inaccessible.
Those who wake them
approach with shaky steps
and touch them
as a man might touch a wound.
They shrivel up,
pull back into themselves
like snails,
and offer only their empty faces
to the passing lights.

translation by Elisavietta Ritchie

Summer's End

Pack summer away
in a carton of straw,
in a sand palace, a poppy's cup,
in the wind's embrace.
But pack it so loosely
that in winter when you're alone
it will escape
from time to time
like some fragrance or a forgotten name.
Like a healing sign.

translation by Linda Pastan and Graham W. Reid

PETAR BOŠKOVSKI

Visits from the Dead

Visits from the dead take their toll.
All prayer is useless, incense a bitter haze.
You boil in your own blood. Pincers tweeze the soul.
A stranger exacts payments, and you pay.

Some return with a generous mission in mind.
Then the ash blossoms, but the flower smokes from fear.
Wine and bread arrive, but a hot breath scorches you.
If you gave from an empty pocket, they fill it.

Some haunt themselves and rise in mortal agony,
heavy and curious to pry out what we know.
Death is lenient, to those he has seized.

And the dead take such liberties—always they impose
on our sleep and time. Here they are, the capable dead.
Only thus can they find their repose.

imitation by Milne Holton and Margaret Gibson from a translation by Graham W. Reid

Drum Beat

You beat in our blood
you knit us tight
you let blood speak.

From an unknown age
you bring before us
a woman in black.

The healing pulse
of your voice
unbinds our souls' beauty

77

and the devil of black despair
is beaten swiftly down,
his gambit doomed

his fifes are caught up
in the spell of rich old wine.
New rebellions are in the waters.

Throughout the wedding is heard
the pulse of the dead's tread;
the bridegroom gives it room.

But what can we think to say
to that woman in black
who knows the veins of fire?

Inside our veins, the ache,
the sweet address of old hills,
the epiphany of sound is within us.

They will never die,
never,
these syllables of time.

imitation by Margaret Gibson from a translation by Graham W. Reid

Little Scars

The first is a spear of cut wheat
The second a ripe husk of sweet basil
The third a sprig of ripe camomile
The fourth a little bird seized by flight
The game goes on with seven eight nine

How tempting they were, other peoples' cherry trees
Way up there in the hedgerows
But what was the attraction of the innocent birds' nests
In the old forest

78

PETAR BOŠKOVSKI

Sometimes I hung upside down
From the top of the highest tree
Took pieces of the horizon in my eyes
And I gave it back brand new to my birds

We also had a frisky horse
Whose reins got tangled by the wind
And then there was a fat and furious tomcat
Zealously committed to the natural state

For a filched fruit, apricot, apple, or pear
We would chase each other for days on end
Ally, brother, sister, cousin
Forever seeking the ripest of all the green fruits

On my face red roses flourished
All over my body, and their sharp roots
Pushed themselves down right into my heart
One time a man I didn't know until that moment
Thrust himself suddenly
Between my anguish and my tears

Did he say then,
Or do I imagine it now,
Let me have those marvelous little scars
And he bore those scars away

Often at certain times
That child comes to lead me
The length of the land that loves me

The game goes on with seven eight nine.

translation by Heddy Reid

PETAR BOŠKOVSKI

Summer Romance

Close to their white baskets
They've spread their dripping shifts
How did they dare?

They started out to gather raspberries
But the river enticed them
Down in the village what would they say if they knew?

The sand with burning eyes
Prickles their flesh
Arousing a sweet rage

An old man passing through the wood watches
Nodding his head
As though remembering an old tale

Perhaps in their tickling and teasing the girls
Imagine a boy in their midst
In the village what would they say if they knew?

There they stand in the shadowed water,
Three young girls, nudes,
Which the eddies painted, entranced.

To the devil with the eddies
Them and their amorous cries
And their hands too weak to make good

The white shifts are drying
And Summer falls to its knees
Shuddering with love

What would happen in the village if they knew?

translation by Heddy Reid

PETAR BOŠKOVSKI

Ravine I

To look at it from the side
One could say through it
Flows the green of the forest

But down the slopes stones
Have rolled into its sunken bed
And have drunk the water to the last drop

From a sun on fire
Fall pieces of flame
Onto the shell of the tortoise

Raising his head
The snake sets out to pursue
A terrorized lizard

I whistle with four fingers
A flood of echoes pounds the slopes
There is no one, no one

Strange mosaics on the sand
Are the souvenir of the last trickle
They are no consolations

Only tears of the clouds
Will be able to revive
Its dried-out hope.

translation by Nancy Marks

PETAR BOŠKOVSKI

Ravine II

We have seen clouds coming
And somewhere beyond the horizon
The sky turning to paste

For the love of God, call back the children
Who go on playing
Along the shores

The sun's torch has wavered
The people have fled in all directions
Sky and earth are blended together

And suddenly we heard it coming
Stones burst into laughter, they cry out
Maddened by the play of the water

The hills open their veins
You are frightened, you watch
Their heads roll and are shattered

Laced with the blood of the earth
Water flows always more savage
Defiling its bed

A man who was running in a greatcoat
Stops suddenly, abandons the gesture
There is no longer a bridge, it is destroyed

The disaster of village and of earth
Gives way to a tale
The aged recount legends

And standing silent beneath the rain
The men pray to God
To spare them the worst.

translation by Nancy Marks

JOZO T. BOŠKOVSKI

Loneliness

The plane tree stands alone in thought
as if in mourning
in this solitude
People pass
but no one notices it
I too walk the path
and stop under its branches
from which dry bark has fallen
in its battle
with time
I form a funnel with my hands
and shout
so that it can hear me
It should stop its mourning
because it has lived alone
in the wind
because it too
did not belong
and because it was left
to the elements.

translation by Herbert Kuhner and Duško Tomovski

Children's Spring Games

The child is the turbulence of the new day
that rushes through the depths of spring
Green field
Green tide
Green sound
Green foam
The child beats the horse with a twig and a flower

JOZO T. BOŠKOVSKI

The horse swings its mane and spreads sunlight over joy
Green field
Green tide
Green sound
Green foam
The youth rides the horse
so that he can find his dream
in high mountains
in the breeding place of the sun.

translation by Herbert Kuhner and Duško Tomovski

PETRÉ M. ANDREEVSKI

The Fourth Letter

Already a year without you, without myself,
already a year an object of gossip
with its wailing voice of professional mourners.
The eyes do not find me, the body doesn't receive me,
and I begin to live as if I had no weight.
My distant thought flashes above the cities,
and my language has only your first name.
I revive you in all the photographs, since I cannot
       find you living—
you the equation between my body and my soul.
In the long year of our separation
I see the causes of all the wars.
You've hid all the bright light under your eyelashes,
(wavering like a sheaf of rye in the wind)
neither the road I travel, nor the dream I dream,
neither the end, the beginning, nor the earth to find you,
and I fall asleep with you, and I awake alone.
A whole year I roam the sad Macedonia,
choosing the words that would celebrate you everywhere,
you my balsam and sugar, you my future joy
keeping alive all my illnesses.
A whole year I keep coming back to you
on rereading your letters,
a whole year as empty as an empty water mill,
like the moon that hollows itself out at midnight crossroads,
a whole year to defend myself against myself,
like the ice that defends itself against its own tenderness,
a whole year you without me, I without myself.

translation by Charles Simic

This and the following poem are from a cycle of poems entitled "Love Letters." ED.

PETRÉ M. ANDREEVSKI

The Fifth Letter

I looked for you in textbooks, among the centuries,
in ambushes of wind, in small fetters of winter,
in the elusive blush of the horizon at sunset,
in the incomprehensible desire of a tobacco leaf
folded and refolded between the fingers,
in the scattered light of the blind and the dead,
in the balance of days gone by and the nights to come,
in the enslaved souls of the blowers of glass.
I looked for you in the accents of unknown languages,
in unsaddled evenings, empty beds spread in a meadow,
in the surprised primrose behind the ear of a florist,
in the rules of punctuation of children's weeping,
I looked for you in the living hope for unity
of all my dispersed peoples,
in the stem of sorrel, in the useless air
which divides and brings together two neighboring villages,
near the anvil of hot feminine noons,
among the fruit trees pointed toward their seasonal aim,
in the needle that sews together darkness and light.
I looked for you by listening to the buried drum
which is the heart of the sleeping harvester.
I looked for you beyond the sky, in the heavenly molehill,
in the unread electric meter of the extinguished light,
in the assassination of men against men,
in the badly studied steadiness of the four cardinal points,
badly studied and understood like the eternal laziness.
I looked for you in the endless fear of stars
which falling touch nothing in space.
I looked for you, I looked for you everywhere,
I looked for you, and thus, I couldn't help but meet you,
yet I never found you, never found you.

translation by Charles Simic

PETRÉ M. ANDREEVSKI

From *Death of the Guiser*

1

We come from God and the devil,
God and the devil we seek;
better to see than to hear us
for one look at our faces
will show you our poisoned hearts.

So began his merry hour without a clock,
his descent into the night which rose up in him.
The guisers walked ahead of their shadows
like smoke which goes before its fire
and bells jangled about their belts
and a withered light dripped behind them.
And while the fire opened up chambers of air before them
he was pursued by an ominous thought
but there was not a particle of space nor time
to hide from the face of the festival.
They began to conjure him up and he to conjure up
various omens and various ills.

Come you inhabitants who measure the ash,
tomorrow is Twelfth Night—the bogeys call you
before the snowy gates to beg water;
they will cut off your arm or cause sudden pain to your leg.
You fall only to rise again, forgotten for a year.
Tell the bride not to breathe in winter
lest the piled up snows thaw on us;
oh, that we may be nowhere, that we may be with her!
. . . .

3

What did you seek, hovering, a shadow among shadows,
why seek out the guisers from the upper villages?
You came upon cold earth in your breast
and you knew: there could be no departure without a death.

87

PETRÉ M. ANDREEVSKI

Why seek such a night torn from the darkness
to gouge out your body like water from mole tracks?
You found yourself, a remnant of the fray:
warm dogwood berries dripping on the snow from your heart
and the dark yarn which the wind spins from your breath.
It was not a pretense but a deception
that you wished to live a bit longer in secrecy;
how could you have known that it would only prolong the pain?
Think of days which will dawn for you
who mingle with us yet are distanced from all.
The day will come to us again but where will you go?
You have found what you sought; the guisers will guise
without you, but now:

>Think of the grass, mow mirages,
>be borne on midnight birds hand over hand,
>set time against time in the storm,
>see the wolf and seek his tracks,
>guard pregnant darks in dim woods,
>roam through the frosts and blow the fires,
>lead a donkey, ride a broomstick,
>keep company with the dead, deal out for the living.

4

You thought: my horse,
my worn-out and sad horse
will have no one to shoe him,
to lead him to water and to pasture,
to put his foot in the stirrup.
And you thought: my axe,
my cold and troubled axe
will have no one to wake and wash it,
no one to leap over it and anger it;
and the fruit trees will have no one to ask them
whether they bear, no one to answer
or bind the golden St. Peter's Day wreaths;
and in me there will be no one to caress

PETRÉ M. ANDREEVSKI

the birth-giving mornings and unharnessed evenings;
and the fire will have no one to praise it
or to guard and fan it for the coming year;
and the wood will have no one to remember it,
no one to repeat the tale of the false blossom
and I'll have nowhere to come back from
into the divine and sad divining:

> The sparrow hawk grew angry among the warp and the woof,
> hurry, hurry and she mastered the sky,
> she wrote no letter and yet reached you,
> lay down in your head and grasped your heart;
> she entered three times and came out six
> and whatever the disturbance of wings
> her wings fluttered and she chased you from sleep.
> . . . .

6

White snow and a black raven spied him out in a deaf time,
and from his hands they took the dry wand
and from the wand the magic in the sleeping sap.
And a murmur of mad bumblebees and crickets
emptied his heart and in it, tomorrow,
water will be able to come to itself.
A hidden ember or a distant light
going out in the depths of his soul
quietly chilled him like a fallen snowflake.
The air was a mirror for his last sigh
and in that sigh his sky was ruined
like a verandah, or like a tower of the blown dandelion.
He shrunk away from the snow which embraced him
and death took him like a nap.

> And when the day began to break
> when the morning appeared,
> they found his soul in the icicles
> twisted in two, in three.

translation by Myra Sklarew and Graham W. Reid

PETRÉ M. ANDREEVSKI

The Fire

You begin to steal from your own house
But out of her you cannot escape
And so for the first time you become visible

You existed existed
In everything you devoured
In everything that devoured you

Praising their death
Men run from you
Not knowing that they carry you within themselves

In all the beds you preserve love
You who are its flag and its soldier

You haul our water to the sky
But without her you cannot return
In each thing you do what you know least

Since you do not know where you come from
Whether out of stone earth or rot
In which you grow smaller the deeper you enter

Everyone you pursue keeps you imprisoned
While on his bones you transplant your flower
As he lies dying as he still possesses you

Oh you double rainbow and evil goodness
You kill the one you defend
So that watching you we weep over nothing

translation by Charles Simic

90

VERA BUŽAROVSKA

The Old Street

On leaving you, I promised to return
to your dusty eyes of stone,
your heart of silence,
I'm your unnatural child
inside a hoop of vice.
But I am coming back
to feel the heat
of your decrepit body,
your creaking bones
and your low roofs.
I'm coming back, I'll take your warmth
to follow me however far
and warm my solitude.

translation by Elisavietta Ritchie and Eugene Prostov

Old Things

This day came burdened
with former days:
with the murmurs of brooks,
with the steepnesses of mountains,
with the moss and lichen of years.
Yet it is simply another day,
an ordinary day;
it has brought nothing new.

translation by Milne Holton and Vera Bužarovska

JOVAN KOTEVSKI

In Spring

As though we had opened the doors
winter has left a heavy load
on the roof beams. The earth burns.
The sun gilds the young bullocks' horns,
the sound revives me.
Far off you wish me to love and die
to love even the child's silvery cry.
Lost to the sunless side, returning
for your ring, my bride,
emerging in the wake of old memories.

translation by Graham W. Reid

Love and Death

We were lost in love
she and I
since yesterday we began to play at death.
The gods hid themselves
from our nakedness.
We dug a heart out of a heart
and our mutual pain
molded us into lovers
in the evening fires of autumn.

Give birth! The earth bears . . .
and we give birth like Eve.
With our long hair
we bind the wounds
of those who've played
at love and death since yesterday
Grass shrivels in the autumn river.

JOVAN KOTEVSKI

Water flows over stones.
Earth flows, heaven flows.
Wind whistles from the flames.
A child cries, earth, stone.

translation by Herbert Kuhner and Graham W. Reid

JOVAN STREZOVSKI

Sun and Mist

Golden mist rises over space
and reveals the richness which it hides
The sun is a golden peacock that walks on grass
It drinks golden water from a golden spring

The nightingale opens a golden chest with its beak
and sends a shrill cry to the heavens
bringing madness to all those who hear it
and the peacock seeks salvation in this madness

Everything I touch I touch fearfully
I am enraptured by this golden brightness
Golden powder drifts down from the trees above
They stand in a golden path auguring my end

translation by Herbert Kuhner and Duško Tomovski

Sleeping Angel

The rain falls, like the rain of the old time,
Like always, the sun drinks water,
Settling to darkness it lights the sky,
And the angel sleeps, sleeps.

Centuries roll past bare stones in the river,
And in them we travel imagined roads;
With each step we expand eternity,
And the angel sleeps, sleeps.

Beneath the angel our times burn on;
The angel would compound the sun's color.
Above him the sun is a jewel;
There the bright doves multiply.

94

Don't wake the angel from his dream;
He has the heart and soul of an old plant;
Let him drink the magic light;
He has gone to look for lost time.

translation by Carolyn Kizer, Milne Holton, Herbert Kuhner, and Danica Cvetanovska

Orpheus of Infinity

Even in silence
Your mind continues: a voice.
Each word expends life,
Love of fire, of the road, of song.
You are consumed in your own flame.

This slow suicide is proof
That you believe in miracles.
As you travel that evil road
You are true to the death.

You surrender to the temptations of distance,
And you are transported.
You are seduced into betrayals;
The infinite begins early for you.

Your soul becomes barren
Like a dried-up river.
Neither prayer nor ritual can save you;
The bottomless pit that waits
Is your earth.

imitation by Milne Holton from translation by Herbert Kuhner and Duško Tomovski

MIHAIL RENDŽOV

I Think of You

I think of you and put you in a word
The word begins to breathe
A bird flies into your eyes
while I write your name

I think of you and put you in a seed
The seed begins to grow, to bloom
I watch you tremble like a milk doe
while the stars fly from love

I think of you and put you in a book
The book begins to breathe . . .

translation by Graham W. Reid

Summer

1

Raise your arm, Bella. My shadow aches shoulder high.
Leaves light up our fingers. My kindled breath weighs me down.
I come out myself. Twice I replace my tiredness
by dusk. A black patch grows
over my throat, while birds enflame the sky.
Look, we're bursting both of us in this blueness.
Our tongues go blue. Cracked in the heat
I feel eyes on fire, our brows burn doubly.

2

Raise your arm, Bella.
Summer mourns prayerless.

translation by Graham W. Reid

MIHAIL RENDŽOV

Summer's End

I am left. Summer dies on our palms.
You dream, Bella. Heat burns on the hill.
You don't know that the years sprout. Branches
prick your brow. You wait.
We are weary of the center. Morning bears
three and thirty yellownesses and frenzies.
Other pupils grow in our eyes. And there is
another rainbow for the scythes. At night
in my hands I shatter your lightness. Bella, we are alone.
We are the mound that's left behind the wattle fence.
This morning we seem taller by a shoulder
and older by a summer.

translation by Graham W. Reid

RADOVAN PAVLOVSKI

In a Star Only

Like a pearl out of a shell
A starfish shines to sailors . . .

I have become a body for my thoughts,
I am the road between stars,
and now I stand up in time.
If the sleepers are searching
for a road between stars,
now I stand up in time.
If the sleepers are searching
for a cure for their sleep,
now the lost time can speak.

Along forgotten roads
a forgotten people
will come,
searching for their own tracks.
If they don't find them
they will become birds
and sing of them.
If the sun disappears,
they will dive deep into the earth
and claw up the sun.
Only in a star
will they find the star.

translation by Milne Holton and Graham W. Reid

RADOVAN PAVLOVSKI

Potter's Song

Horses carrying pottery[1]
field flowers in their eyes
trot by;
their path is paved
with sunshine and moonlight.

There's a song in us
of hard earth and distant roads,
and our roof
is the color of dreams.
That vase under the sky
has a girl's shape and voice;
thirsty kings will fight
for this earthen cup.

It isn't brittle earth
that breaks when the cup breaks;
it's a flickering star that crashes.

Horses loaded with wheat
field flowers in their eyes
trot by;
their path is paved
with sunshine and moonlight.

translation by Herbert Kuhner and Duško Tomovski

Climate and Lyre

Where is the sky born?
Or will my triumphs be recorded
Only in my sad eyes which face Olympus?

---

1. The poet almost certainly has in mind the pottery carried by horse and donkey to the pottery market in Resen, a small town in southern Macedonia. ED.

The seasons change the climate, O my soul,
Like gamblers dealing cards.
Why do you echo randomly in my ear
This note of sorrow?

I don't know if my country really needs me
But I give myself to her with words
As if I were an unknown warrior.
Color suddenly invades the void;
With a bronze resonance, a poplar leaf
Drops from its stem.

A harsh word breaks my lyre in two.
Where are your lightnings, sky?
The tree, in its grief for the bird,
Begins to resemble the bird.

translation by Carolyn Kizer and Bogomil Gjuzel

Weapons

Who knows how often,
weapons left in the rain and the sun
cause shrieking in the dreams
of generations and nations.

Under them lies dead earth,
the sky above them is a poem of mourning
for that unfortunate game of the mind.
Who knows when

and by whose hands these weapons
were left in disinfectant or in wounds.
It's impossible to believe
that they'll survive to be used again.

translation by Herbert Kuhner and Duško Tomovski

RADOVAN PAVLOVSKI

The Flood

1

The dark blue drum of the Flood
beats upon ridges
In the house on the shore
the people are frightened
The sky will fill up our heads
with ponderous water
throughout the beautiful world
may the race be buried under earth
Complete your flight, bird
don't carry weight
We are killed as we stand
I was scared by the quick sprouting of seed
in sinister granaries
And on the seventh day there appeared
the terrible shadow of the Flood.

2

Sharp thunder of heavy summer
My horse runs from dark to light fields
Seeing him I fill my song with fear
The froth at his mouth terrifies me
Sky falls in hatchets
which cut this white noon into night
O my God my black-headed horse
hooves strike rock
sparks shower
and set me on fire
I am spending the night in an animal's lair
Bushes converse overhead
on deep waters
I have a star
which shows you mean to drown us.

RADOVAN PAVLOVSKI

3

My horse is in the ninth heaven
All I have first sown gave birth to tears
A cross for the bread and cold wine
The fearful shadow of the Flood appears in the skies
My bead will not let me sleep
The water wants me drowned.

translation by Elisavietta Ritchie and Eugene Prostov

Drought

Bent doubled-up cattle
bellow powerfully for each lost horn
The sky doesn't listen

The birds strung in a circle
make a hard flight in the air
We hold palms upturned for prayer

The clock ticks
the scorching heat of grasses
The wind hardly brings two or three drops of rain

Cracked and bloodied feet
can kill everything on the road

Marking a black thread
the ants bury themselves deeply
The belated rain begins to fall
Our homes are open to the flood
My round body aches in the water
My killed bird does not fly through the air
I can open the window
and cry myself mad.

translation by Vasa D. Mihailovich

Maja

1

It was like a curse when I saw the stars in daytime:
I was approaching you, my hands full of darkness and speech,
Like a vagrant I feared sleeping in roads
for the great ants would tear at my skin
but you lifted me in air
I perched in your tower like a bird
and my soul quenched the crowd's thunder and lightning.
Then we chose a wide place, of flowers and bells.
I came there as a reaper, full of whistling,
you came full of fruit.
All around us were thieves' tracks.
We lost dawn through our fingers.
The crickets stored the beauty of flowers against winter.

It was like a curse when I saw the stars in daytime:
I was clearing a road to protect you
In the air were the cries of our children
I destroyed other good things so I could see our pure treasure
with its fiery heart.
When you were coming I spread my arms on the ground.
Proud bells shook the sky
scented with thyme.

2

Give back to the waters the blue stone
where grass flowers and tides are enclosed.
My heart ripened with the wheat.
In the afternoon the sun breathed life into the sickness of the rooms,
I set out the flower to breathe air. Heroes were struggling in the fields,

Maja is a European goddess of fertility. ED.

everywhere was the smell of war, invisible war. And then a wedding.
For Maja and I were born king and queen,
wed by tide, destroyed by rain.
A red fruit lit up the bed, a shadow from the forest
lingered in the window.
It was the shadow that hid us when we hid in the forest,
That was the time when the golden dogwood blossoms fell on the snow;
that was the month of our love.
The moon like a black nun
wandered through tall flowers. Where was the center of things?
O Maja, dew and fire,
may the bread rise, the milk overflow
on the fire, It is useless. A ghost-actor
wanders lost on the roads.

3

I smell the warrior roses of Samuel,
reaper of wars.
My body will vanish in dreams,
but my dark blue whistling will remain
to frighten the birds.
In the ashes I can see
wood from that forest.
Snakes enter the house with summer,
they hold beneath their tongues
the voices of the dead.
In the tall wheat is a boat
that will sail away with the floods.
Child who cries,
your father is the youth who wanders around at noon
and writes poems about the sun.
I ask that you may sleep on the hill among the dark violets,
that you may see the sun up close
and the healing color of pollen from mating bees.
The days are getting shorter; blindness comes;
now love is a lost urge,

herb, smoke from a dead fire.
The children sleep in the corn, their lips whistle,
they object to the birds
that pass over in their dreams.
I, a youth on the edge of sleep,
kill the angry roses.

imitation by Milne Holton from translations by Bogomil Gjuzel and Graham W. Reid

The Road to the Mountain

I will discover the red stone of thunder
O dried herbs
I will roll you into a cigar
and light you from the lightning
The sky-bird is an evil sign
Do not drink nocturnal water
my unshod horse
you will not carry me home
Because magic was buried with the foundation stone of my house
I tripped over subterranean winds
I will lie in the starry gardens on the hill
in a bed of roses
Let them light a candle on my head
and let the hail beat me flat as wheat
I was ready to take root
but my mole came
My unshod horse, you will drop dead from my weight
The cattle bar my way
The sky is scorched by lightning
The weeping stones rush toward my head
I won't reach home before the first cockcrow.

translation by Carolyn Kizer and Vasa D. Mihailovich

105

IV

The Avant-Garde

Bolen Dojčin—The Sick Hero

1

The White City sleeps under the cover of fog and snow.
In its swaddling clothes the universe continues its agonizing birth;
One cannot hear the cries of newborn children.
Posterity is forgotten; the cradles do not rock;
The black seed is buried; fresh wine
Ferments the evil blood which will crow in another time.

The green bronze gates are silent,
Wet with the warm tongue of mother-fog.
No one knows where the stand the ramparts,
Whence cometh the fields and the wide world.
The caravans have arrived and are locked in the taverns
(Camels still groan from the burden).
The inns are invisible, wrapped in warm breath and white smoke;

In the wine now one seeks his own blood,
In the bread strength and new oaths.

Wherever there is death there are limits,
There is the chain of stillness; there cries mean the end;
And no one calls back death from there with his screams.
Therefore I am lying ill in the tower of air,
Dampening the glass with my breathing.
I leave my teardrop to wander alone.

2

We lie asleep above an abyss. Each has his own hell,
In each nerve, to endure and to survive.
One after the other the candles are lit there
To make it brighter and warmer.

Like Blažé Koneski's, Gjuzel's "Bolen Dojčin" is a modern version of a very old Macedonian folk narrative, of the same name, which is to be found in the Appendix. ED.

In our fingers, in breathing one limited world
In which again confusion and stuffiness dominate
(One cannot live with the thought
That nothing moves behind our backs)
Even what kills us
Is soiled by the familiarity of our own hands.

Stop squinting through the navel in that dot of a sky
From that trodden womb of nutritious fogs!
We wait, and we scratch for our birth, and yet we are not born.
Thus the fruit perishes in the womb
Without the separation that must come from our own hand.
That law is cruel which says we must deliver ourselves,
That we alone create our doom and peril,
But it is more dreadful to bear
The curse of an unborn germ.
Had not our mother and country been cursed by us
Then upon us they would make double curse.

Therefore I lie ill in this tower of air
Deeply wrapped in the folds of fog and snow
Waiting for that day promised by my fates,
The new curse to unlock the world
And then the final stroke to receive it.
I have waited for the salutary lark,
Have scratched about in the parental dark,
Have trodden upon those miraculous wells and plants,
Have spotted the weapon with stains of blood,
And again I lie ill in the White City, in this city of grief,
And again nothing comes to happen
Nothing to make me use my strength, consecrated
To the birth of so many dawns,
To the rising of the birds
Blinded by rainbows of blood.

3
In my dream I touched bottom;
To be nothing and nothing more. I was nothing; I foretold nothing.

BOGOMIL GJUZEL

But even in the last pores of earth,
I found air to be breathed.
And it is this same air of the White City
(Which whitens this city and blackens the earth);
Like a gimlet my fate drills
Through the hard life to make this easy poem.
Regrettably, no one can stop it.
Let my joy utter its cry,
Let the word sing out its law.

Oh, to be nothing—only to measure that word!
And to measure the other—to be all and to measure all!
But even then there is no peace,
For we are born to be without measure,
To touch all and to be like none.
I, who touched bottom, dropped the sword
From my hands, soared like a bird in this fog.
To reach many hearts and be back milky again I sought hearts; I sought
    milk again.
Broken in blood I can confirm this
(Gladly would I sign away my soul).
I mourn the fallen bird.

But tears are blood, and I am broken
I must be as I am or change;
I must be familiar or strange.
Each is minted in the coin of his time
But blow, and that shape is no more;
Even metal can be changed by sighs
Or, cruel, hold shape,
to be used for a kiss or for war.
And it will no more lose its strength
Then we our desires.
We are the same as metal.

Yes, the metal or you—silence will say yes
To us or to metal the silence will say nothing
Neither kiss nor weapon,

BOGOMIL GJUZEL

Neither air nor the worm, heart nor emptiness
In which it is bred like a mushroom,
Neither birth-light nor grave-dark.
The mouth filled with air or with fertile earth
Out of it will spring a new Samuel,
Only he can pull down the silence;
There is only one choice: to be or to die.
I only am here to choose,
Mute voter in deaf fog in a White City.

Good night, fate, I've done,
See you tomorrow; there's always another day.

imitation by Carolyn Kizer and Milne Holton from a translation by Howard Erskine-Hill

From *Troy*

The gates of the city burst open,
and in came the wind—like someone
just freed from siege,
like the empty soul of a conqueror,
who afterwards expects nothing—
a senseless, idle gust,
sauntering along the streets,
wearied by their corners,
a beggar's breath,
looking for warmth and bread crusts.
It was the cobblestones that moaned,
the palaces that shivered.

Gjuzel studied literature at the University of Edinburgh in 1964 and 1965, and his earliest poetry, while reflecting his own experiences in his homeland in the years after the war, also shows the influence of T. S. Eliot and of the Scots poet, Edwin Muir (1887–1959). ED.

And the wind brought people,
who had let their ploughs rust;
solitary people tilling the sky,
reaping the harvests of summer nights,
the fat grain of the early stars,
leaving it all unwinnowed.
Instead they used swords;
their ploughing was of bodies,
their furrow cut to the heart;
they plucked out hearts like stump roots,
they burst gall bladders.
with livers they fed the vultures on their shoulders.
At the last they rolled away the skulls
like stones for building.
For building there was never time.

Mothers were torn from their children;
both milk and cry dried up.
Streets were watered by broken pipes,
pulsing like ruptured arteries.
Sacrifices were hurried;
the hope was for nothing
but to turn the temples into sties
and to provoke the usual stench.
The wind unraveled the bell ropes and the flags,
and, with its whirling tail,
it passed like a broom through the city
and struck the gong of the sun.

imitation by Milne Holton from a translation by Bogomil Gjuzel and Howard Erskine-Hill

BOGOMIL GJUZEL

Black Came the Plague

The plague came decked out in a silken coach
Not like a gipsy in rags or a scaly old crone
But like a beauty on a caparisoned horse,
Under a veil lifted by angel-eunuchs;
Beauty that scorches,
With a ship like the fire dragons spew,
Like a tribute drying up the blood.

A black sea-galley.
Lower the flags from your towers and strongholds,
Lock your shutters and gates,
Shut yourselves in behind your eyelids
Still it will spy you out
With the inexorable worm in the air.

Houses crumble worm-eaten,
Clothes fall apart like cobwebs,
Scuttling through alleyways rats die
Caught in flight.

Changed by fate into a stork I saw all this
From the chimney—how my people die,
How the threshold crumbles;
Changed demonlike into a grain of millet I saw it,
Changed into a wizard who rides on a broomstick.

Show yourselves, Christian leaders,
With fire and the sword of salvation
Kindle and burn, crush the tribes,
For I saw the spy passing secretly
To visit you, changed into nothing,
More devil than I.

translation by Edward Gold and Graham W. Reid

BOGOMIL GJUZEL

Sultry Time

1

The lightning brings forth no fruit.
It is only a wound in the sky,
which is left like a bloodied slaughterhouse,
like a battlefield after battle.

The rain falls engenders no birth,
only the headless bodies of the stillborn.
And the house is transparent
like a ghost.
This piece of paper, like a terrified mouse,
rushes straight into the cat's maw of time.

The sound of thunder tells us nothing;
it only plays tricks with our ears,
and it digs deeper furrows
in the pit of our bottomless pain.

2

Light is forbidden us;
The flashes are underground fire-rivers,
Dark bands of current between poles.

The lost stars are black fireflies
which the air presses down.
They bring the diseases to the roots.
Only these seeds do they spread with their fire.

At the end, we are fed by ashes.
Our bellies split, having been filled with stones.

translation by Carolyn Kizer, Milne Holton, and Graham W. Reid

From *Journey to the City of Lenguel*

1

I came to the City of Lenguel
A sigh captured me
I pushed back walls
And with the bricks of dream scratched out a dwelling.
My soul came in through the chimney
And my cry rose over the towers.
I was slapped by the windy plain
Ripped open by boar-toothed citizens;
I'll pick up the weathercocks
And move south, singing of migrations.

2

The growing City of Lenguel is no match,
Cannot fill the spaces in my dream;
The sky sits on the roof and begins its daily round.
I stain the tower with blood,
I migrate with my song, settle down in my hunger
Among bricks of that dream.
With horns of slaughtered boars
The north blows its trumpets at the gates.
The plain disappears.
Now there is no nest for my cuckoo offspring.
It is a season of nomads, dust and sunshine.
O save the road the sun has covered with lead,
The road to the City of Lenguel, the lead city!

. . . .

Lenguel, or Lengyel, is an archeological site in western Hungary, where evidence has been found of settlements of the fifth millenium B.C. unlike their neighbors and bearing resemblances to those on or near the Adriatic. These findings give rise to speculation that around that time there were migrations from the Adriatic coast (now the Yugoslav coast) to the basin of the Sava River. ED.

5

Knee-deep in the City of Lenguel
I hear the pealing of lead bells;
The road's corroded body,
The river's eye swollen from sleeplessness,
Blind thoroughfares and nomads
Burn into me.
By horse lies dead on the cobbles.

I'll turn away, destroyed on towers
And crenellations, from the jawless skull of the north
I'll set fire to the nest of snakes,
My birthplace in the south,
With a new song and migration.

I put out the sun, fall asleep;
None shall know I was born
In a season of cruel nomads.

translation by Carolyn Kizer and Arvind Krishna Mehrotra

Odysseus in Hell

1

Get lost,
you lotus-eater, disheveled wanderer,
I'm just a boy asleep on the wind's corners
hiding in sand castles;
stop pursuing me!
Does one ever get away?
O.K., I'll turn into a worm:
All I need is a dark night, fresh soil,
two words for my song,
none for my love.
I married secondhand Hydrae
they were whipped on the bare steppes, they danced.

117

I placed an order for freedom
O which sun made me a beggar?
I don't want women
I want hot springs
sharp pinlike winds
to lie on
(I who roamed
the wind's corners).
I want the rituals of mating
performed in young woods
where the sun is plentiful.
May your own blood tear you to pieces,
bitter wanderer of the planets,
stupid Graeco-Macedonian,
let drums hound you out of the mountains,
let marshes and traps swallow you.
Get lost!

> *And while bells at the crossroads*
> *announced a war, condemned Odysseus*
> *fell backward into hell.*

2
> *I am Odysseus, a Graeco-Macedonian.*

Odysseus rolled down the morning
and stopped to break through noon,
he blew out hell's candles,
his thoughts had cheated him.

3
Both hell and I
are being stolen by shadows
I shall disappear when night wears
its freshly ground stars;
on a white night the blood
looks thicker.

Timid hell was being built
by some old bums with girders
of hard wind.

You walk on music with bare feet,
the wind dresses you in transparent skins,
you are a citizen of the world,
man of white wines and sailcloth.
The sands—my innumerable parents
on the old evangelic beach—save me
with hot pliers
and their brazier of death.
The misery
to mate in hell
with reeds and sterile dragonflies.
At crossroads I still make the sign.

4

Between the Grecian and Macedonian lands
there is no one
yes, O yes, no one.
White villages, sad horses,
keep heaping stars on me
or I'll vanish.

Don't think of those wretched horses.
The villages of Taurus and Crystal:
Two green eyes. Swamps.

The tall dry grass of the steppes
killed the old men;
the Hydrae undid
the knots of the souls.
Odysseus nibbled at the road
of the unshod horses,
the earth got smaller
and Odysseus belched with satisfaction
yes, O yes, bravery.

119

The village of Taurus
enters the sky,
the village of Crystal
enters the earth to be changed
into a light year:
Two green eyes. Caverns.

Higher up the Arctic boils
the scents lead
to a white village
razed by longing.
Someone wearing a farmer's cape
stands against the horizon.
Darkness stops breathing
and lecherous souls dance
to the whips of precocious Hydrae.

> *Give all the new ones to Odysseus,*
> *the true Graeco-Macedonian.*

The land reduced to a tenant farmer.

Go still higher, Odysseus,
you are the fastest runner
between the wastelands of Greece and Macedonia.
Tear down those ambiguous Hydrae
so they won't crack their whips
or suffer
for a soul that isn't there
for a road corroded by the horses' vomit
between the wastelands of Greece and Macedonia.

The villages of Taurus and Crystal:
Two worlds. Blue violets.

5

Dry branches and thin men
protect you from the sun,

unless you melt it
by going near.

> *You poured acid*
> *on this coin*
> *as it led you down the road.*

6

In the end
he spread out the sun
broke the light
threw away the dark.
He was not married.

The Hydrae still mourn him,
the steppes continue the raids.

> *He lit a fire and vanished.*

The women waited at the crossing.
The strange
Graeco-Macedonian roads
settled themselves in his body.
It's time to run away from yourself, Odysseus.

A song and the sun torn apart
was all that remained.

translation by Arvind Krishna Mehrotra

Satanael

Boredom. Neither day nor night
You came to the surface, a pochard

Satanael, according to the traditions of certain Macedonian and Bulgarian sects, was the elder son of God, Christ being the younger. ED.

And he saw you. But then why dive back
Not frightened, just surprised—were you?—
At being seen
Why obey him, dig, bring up
The earth in your mouth?
Shame on you and your vanished sea's
Transformation.

So you spat out a rock for two.
After which nightmare or daydream
Did you decide to push him in his sleep?
The rock grew up on an island
Not surprised? Be quick
Or the earth will outrun you
You raced in four directions to push him
There was no shore, only the extending earth.
You cursed and made the sign of the cross.

How come in an endless world
You spoke with that sweet-shitting bee, his spy
Of course you saw her, but riding
The goat you had to mumble to yourself
She went and taught him how to knead
To whip out mountains and valleys;
The earth, sensing danger, turned into a hedgehog.
Mad at your stupid rebellion
You dropped half your name.

What next? Leave holes in the first human
So he can fill them with healing herbs
Make yourself a clay wolf to bite
And maim you; rule over the dead, limbless snake.
Before Adam tills ask him to sign the lease
Advise an angel or saint
You know they'll take it
Though make sure they get confused
Let him smell the basil leaves and have a son.

. . . that's enough. Now you are spat upon,
Farted at, chased by rabid dogs and stinking torches
Hot-Iron-Face, you go down the black pit.
It's all over
Just confirm where things are
Don't you sometimes think
"What if I hadn't surfaced . . . fallen asleep
Talked to myself like any old fool . . .
If I hadn't allowed him . . . ?"

Sure but then you wouldn't be the fly that survived winter.

translation by Arvind Krishna Mehrotra

Flood at the International Writers' Workshop

Since the sky started crying
I haven't been out-of-doors for thirty-one days:
By now the earth must be a pair of pliers
With tatters of human flesh stuck to its jaws.

I imagine myself on a seesaw, balanced so lightly
That if even an atom fell on it (let alone a bomb)
I would be hurled like a stone from a catapult
Straight back into the trap of Macedonia.

My people, are we God's voracious eye
Suspended in the air like a traffic light
Which, as it blinks, directs the flow of nations?
Right now I'm only that greedy eye of legend
Which, on my side of the scale, outweighs the world.

Gjuzel spent 1972–1973 in residence at the International Writers' Workshop at
the University of Iowa. ED.

BOGOMIL GJUZEL

In the Ark, our elevators work erratically:
Every deck is bursting with trapped livestock!
On the first floor, insects have turned into neurons
Without any owners:
On the second, saurians form a mythic chain
To swallow each other so they will all disappear,
Be too feeble to achieve total consummation;
On the third floor, the mad vegetarians
Roaring with hunger, lay waste the frigidaires;
On the fourth, the carnivorous flowers
Make plans to devour God;
On the fifth floor, this lone Macedonian
Mangles their languages, re-creating Babel.

And every line that occurs to me sinks like a plummet
When it should splash about like a happy dog
And, like a dolphin, jump through its trainer's hoop.
But I'm dense when it comes to featherweight words!
The verb should be in a state of constant erection,
In equal readiness to strike, or stroke;
The adjective stick to the noun like a lizard catching flies;
And the noun should swing both ways,
While the conjunction is a universal passkey.

So the sky sobs on, like an hysterical child,
Like the she-dragons of my legends.
The gutters gurgle, and gargle.
The drainpipes are subterranean Mississippis.

The words refuse to swallow us any longer
Now we have set them to quarreling among themselves:
Trying to strangle each other, they bite off their tongues.
They have burned to tell us everything they know,
But, being dumb now, drooling idiots,

Speechlessly, they copulate with rainbows.

translation by Carolyn Kizer

124

BOGOMIL GJUZEL

Professional Poet

The last word, the last hasty swallow

you get up from the table, after your working day
and catch the first bus to the kitchen
you tear off a hunk of bread, inhale the good oven odors
Your body, leaden with weariness, the mold
you cram with rich food
Switch on the set   and inspect the backyard
through another screen   with a wet finger
you flip the pages of the sky.

Nothing will come of nothing.
                           Clematis tendrils
float in the void . . . THEY MUST BE TRAINED ON A TRELLIS
your daughter brings you a chair
The table is set, your wife calls
through the window of a parallel world.

After dinner, you walk in the garden
alone in your pressurized space-suit,
                           stars all around you
even beneath you. Your antennae must be redirected.
the pear tree, newly pruned, requires manure.

Back to the module:
                   Daddy, what does it mean
to be a monster?
                   Suddenly, the chain of command dissolves
bits of paper whirling in free fall
around the table:
                   untouched paper
and your pencil, ominous as a revolver.

translation by Carolyn Kizer

125

SVETLANA HRISTOVA-JOCIĆ

In This Room

When I laugh in this room
Walls move about
And when I continue the watersprites' dance
The ceiling turns into the sky.
When I laugh in this room
The flame in the oil lamp blossoms.
When I mend the arms of the doll
The colors in carpets come alive and dance.
Then I outwit the truth
Of our flesh and our bones.

translation by Elisavietta Ritchie and Eugene Prostov

From *Crucified*
A set of lyrics

A white bud on the ash's horn
The whilrpool beneath on fire
The cramping frost above
Where shall I put it?
I lack God's force
I am the pain within this circle
The bloody foam is crucified in my throat

The gold horseshoe of love
Leaves torches of rye

translation by Elisavietta Ritchie and Eugene Prostov

KIRIL BUJUKLIEV

We Have Nothing More in Common

We have nothing more in common, have we?
I've become allergic to your rotting face,
Reality flows like clear water dividing us,
And I must return to the blood which beckons me.

Cross where you will, even infect the birds,
Darken others' happiness, break branches,
Even if your malice is but a trick played on the world
Play the queen of reeking corpses.

Drive the woods mad as darkness falls;
Don't give up your empty orgies
I think a new light is being born in my veins
And scorching flames will leap up in my heart.

Tonight, woman, I will finish this poem,
For I have no need of flowers which do not bloom
All is now clear—we have nothing in common;
The living and the dead are worlds apart.

translation by Graham W. Reid

DUŠICA TODOROVSKA

"War Was . . ."

Viper's venom lies heavy in the eye;
The aspen trees are all ashes.
Where are the wooded hillsides?
Where is the heart open like a magnolia?
Where is the laughter in soldiers' clothes?

Helmet, helmet, helmets—
A beetle is peaceful in a pierced skull.
Grass burns under fiery claws,
Shoots out the seed of all the plagues.
Where are the nutshells?
Where is the sleep in the hillocks?
Where is the exhumed soul?

Helmet, helmet, helmets—
Drumsticks beat a dry udder.
Oak roots burrow under the heart.
Whispers dig graves under foliage.
No one is alive among the empty bones.

translation by Elisavietta Ritchie and Eugene Prostov

Echo's Voice

I hid my memory in a white flower;
my body became invisible.
Many girls came to confession,
but I always dreamt of flowers.
I whispered;
my whisper resounded in emptiness.
And I loved;
no one accepted my love.
And I hurt;
but no one eased my hurt.

DUŠICA TODOROVSKA

Narcissus saw himself in my eye;
the milk of the evil nymphs transported him;
he went away with the star of his heart.
That is why, in nine hundred ninety-nine instances,
the sounds of my cries are orphaned.

But I love it, the flower,
pinned through veins to its root.
This is not the odyssey of the gods,
this is not a secret spread in a cave,
this is not a stone thrown into still water,
it is the destiny of a woman's flesh.

translation by Elisavietta Ritchie and Eugene Prostov

ATANAS VANGELOV

The Flower Called Day

1

You can happen on a tree in a wood
and believe it was created just for you.
If there is a river flowing nearby
you look for a link between river and tree:
So you create the religion of the tree
and are astonished by it.
The legend can run backward
and still be true.

Which means
if you hold and know it
you have already gone beyond it.
If you turn away and ignore it
it will bind you to it.

2

River, who turns against me
against my holding in sand,
river, who sprouts in everything called a flower
shatter it with water.
In the end it is all the same,
what can and cannot
be called flower.

If you encounter the strange moment
when you believe what does not exist
the moment is a flower to cure the soul.

translation by Ann Darr and Graham W. Reid

ATANAS VANGELOV

Anatomy of a Flower

When the sun and the spring
(out of need or something)
drew flowers on a tree
suddenly
a bird flew in
for its own reason
the wind rode in
for its own reason
and the rain knocked
as if at a significant door
for its own reason
and finally
the poet arrived too
for his own reason

The bird flies away
(the reason for its coming
is in its song)

The wind rides on
(it has already learned
the language of flowers)

The rain too retreats
(the music for which it came
is recorded in its murmur)

Only the poet wonders
whether on his departure
he has also taken
the bird
and the wind

and the rain.

translation by Vasa D. Mihailovich

131

ATANAS VANGELOV

An Attempt to Explain the Origin of a Flower

Write
this fire is fiercer than the soldier
who subdues the armies of fear
and I
and I will only add that
Flower

Write
That forest is older than your existence
than the burning you know from your blood
older than the one who threatens
to burst out like a star
and I
and I don't know what to add except
Flower

Write
write something comforting
something felt from far away
something to make men search themselves
and I
and I will only add that
Flower

translation by Heddy Reid

ČEDO JAKIMOVSKI

Open Up, Sea

Was it a bright wind that blew up from my dream
Under the warmth it soared like pollen
Now I am the thunderclap of a broken bell
which along invisible roads seeks a promised land
Did I discover you, though, in the secret root
when awake I dream of an unknown Sea.

Sea, firework of water and sand
Sea, child's toy of drunken waves
Did you throw me on the hot sand
I a rotten galley in a net of algae
Half-blind to see a strange diadem
In somebody's eyes which no longer exist.

Woman, are you a thought of a new Noon
darkness in consciousness, golden bird that you are
Unspoken word, magnetic planet
thought which bears me into meaninglessness
when a ray raises me up toward infinity
when awake I dream of the bed of a new Sea?

Or I am a black stone loosened from fatigue
fallen on the shore to quench its thirst
And the Sea stands like a marble statue
Will absence save the fruit
Break up, sky, stir up, foam,
Give me to drink again, Sea, you absent woman.

Does something have to be broken inside
an old apathy fall from the mind
But what will happen if the moment end
and darkness grasp this mad Noon
Oh marvel: a black pain wanders through the heat
and the Sea keeps silent in a vast shell.

Wake up, Sea, sun-filled Poem,
Unheard music, magic of death,

ČEDO JAKIMOVSKI

Fanged darkness beholds me from the mute sky
and writes secret messages on my back
Be playful, water, the booty is in your hands
Sea, unfinished dream, you absent woman.

The road to freedom passes through you
the sailors doze to empty graves
and the coming storm scratches their subconscious
they dream of a wind which doesn't exist
The storm circles lost, alone
Sea, blue woman, open the temple.

Enchanted secret, immobile snake,
break the bonds of the old water
let a whirlwind blow from new metaphors
so that I may sail quietly to my white death
In the whirlpool where the memories turn
to destroy the lighthouse of death with a word.

The words fall like birds' nests
Time is a slave of some golden polyp
To proceed, where . . . The promised star,
before it is born aches hopelessly
Sea, wise woman with cold thighs,
toward whose silence let me float with torn sails.

translation by Ann Darr and Graham W. Reid

PETRÉ BAKEVSKI

Journey to the Colors of the Sky

Before this canvas before this summer
appearing in the drowsy taking flight
of butterflies I would
rest my eyes
in that color in that sky in the flight
of weary birds
toward the lake. The naiads
stretching out in the drawing
on golden sand
the landscape
facing the sun
red I set out for the color of the sky.

translation by Graham W. Reid

Dream at Noon

At noon
I sleep with dreams long and wide
Someone is dreaming in my name
The fire of conversation comes: one
laughs while one
fears silence's long tongue.

Do they converse
of the quiet of the butterflies

The sun grows on a dry branch beneath the summer
What time of day
and year is it

PETRÉ BAKEVSKI

Birds fly across the broad
sight
of a deserted
shore: one fire
laughs and without one
there is fear.

translation by Graham W. Reid

TODOR ČALOVSKI

Way In

You came here to enter completely
But there is always left behind you
Something greater than your dream
You have no time to think of trivialities
for you live in a time that understands you alone
You cannot answer for what pursues you
for you conquer here penetrated on all sides
You don't differentiate the horse's dream from that of the horseman
You could come in without anyone seeing you
be free as long as I don't possess you
For only so is the flight prolonged
For only so does the world go on.

translation by Graham W. Reid

From *Achasfer*

He will pass here too, he will pass now,
without their grasping him, or his seeing me;
and he will be falsehood, and will flee again,
without their catching him, without his ease.

That mad exile pains me,
that fiery pillar raises me aloft;
it holds neither sound nor the wrath of judgment.
What is the offence, strange god?

He stole the morning in his mind;
the day wakes in us without him,
standing like quicksilver on the shore
of dead moons, shining.

Achasfer is Ahasuerus, the Wandering Jew. The first written account of the story attributes it to an archbishop of Armenia, who reported it in England in 1228. ED.

TODOR ČALOVSKI

Vainly we all awaited him here
by the threshold he might have entered;
so we didn't notice when he began to fire
and we fell prostrate behind the infernal bolt.

translation by Graham W. Reid

Seeing Stars

I know
that there behind the last embers
where ashes suffer from vertigo
where all laws of duality are changed
where even the spaces between spaces are swept away
where controlled emptiness
is more dangerous than any imaginable depth,
there is a star,
which can do nothing but collide
with its own light at a shrieking speed
and thus will return the ornaments
from the poem to be by an unborn poet
since it cannot discard anything else.

translation by Milne Holton, Herbert Kuhner, and Duško Tomovski

RADOVAN P. CVETKOVSKI

The Ploughmen of the Moon

In horsehair sacks the ploughmen stash their grain
The broody hen ransacks the sky
pecking at stars above the plain.
While
there where the valley flows
the moon rolls like a golden bowl
thrown into the sky.

With skirts tucked up she runs by the river
playing hide-and-seek with the fish.
At dawn she gilds the willows.
Late she runs over the plain.
With goads the ploughmen chase her through the fields,
fire curses in her eyes—
she leaves her tears on the plain,
her gold in the hedgerows
to gild the handles of the plough the following night.

The ploughmen bury their grain in the night
beat the moon with their goads,
impale her on their ploughshares
to dig their furrows deep.

translation by Ann Darr and Graham W. Reid

Appendix: Ancestors

FOLK POETRY

Bolen Dojčin

The Black Arab has appeared;
He has fallen upon the Solun[1] plain.
He has raised his white tents on the meadows.
He demands tribute from Salonika town:
Two ovens of bread he demands,
A barrel of arak, two barrels of wine,
He demands an uncalved heifer,
A beautiful bride he demands every day,
And for loving every night he demands a young maid
To love and then to destroy.
All maidens must serve their turn.
Now the turn is to young Angelina.
The young Angelina is sweeping her yard,
She is sweeping and great tears are falling.
Her tears are sprinkling the courtyard.
Bolen Dojčin, her brother, observes her,
From his sickbed he looks out of the window:
"So,[2] Angelina, my sister,

"Bolen Dojčin" (the title means "Sick Dojčin," or "Dojčin the Ill One") is one of the oldest of the Macedonian epic songs and has come to stand as the very embodiment of the tradition for a number of Macedonian poets, Blažé Koneski and Bogomil Gjuzel among them. These poets make elaborate and sometimes ironic reference to this poem of honor and revolt in "Bolen Dojčins" of their own.

After a number of raids, Salonika fell to the Ottomans in 1430; one can therefore presume a date of composition for "Bolen Dojčin" as being around that year. ED.

1. "Solun" is the Slav form of "Salonika," as mentioned in our Introduction. ED.

2. "So" here translates the Macedonian phrase, *ajti tebe,* a phrase of ambiguous meaning—sometimes a greeting, sometimes an expletive, sometimes a word of encouragement, lit., "come" or "come on"—in modern Macedonian. It recurs throughout the poem prefatory to speeches. ED.

143

What sorrow has befallen you?
While you're sweeping, your great tears are falling!
Are you weary of sweeping our smooth courtyard?
Or of nursing your poor ailing brother?
Or of binding my sores and my wounds?
Or of making me sickbed gifts?"
"So, Bolen Dojčin, my brother.
I'm not weary of sweeping our smooth yard,
Nor of caring for you, ailing brother,
Nor of binding your sores and your wounds,
Nor of making you sickbed gifts.
Something else is wearying me, brother:
That Black Arab has appeared.
He has appeared below Salonika town,
Near the town, on the Solun plain.
He has raised his white tents on the meadows.
He has gathered the priests and the elders.
Every day two ovens of bread he demands,
A barrel of arak, two barrels of wine,
He demands an uncalved heifer,
Every day he demands a beautiful bride,
and every night a young maiden
To love and then to destroy.
All the maidens must serve their turn.
My turn has come; now they will take me."
Bolen Dojčin answers his sister:
"So now, my sister Angelina,
So this is indeed your misfortune!
Nine years I've lain ill on my bed—
Go open the painted wooden chest,
Take out three hundred ells of the linen,
Take three hundred ells of fine woven cloth,
To bind up my wounds still unhealed from the daggers.
And also take out my keen sabre;
Nine years have gone by since I held it,
And now it is covered with rust.

144

Take my sabre to Umer the Sawsmith,
Let him sharpen it for me on trust.
If I rise from my bed, he'll be well paid.
If I don't, let him give me his blessing."
Then young Angelina stands up
And fetches forth that rusty sabre
And bears it to Umer the Sawsmith.
"So, good day, O Umer the Sawsmith,
In God's name, I pray you, please hear me;
Brother Dojčin sent me with his sabre.
Will you sharpen it for him on trust?
If he gets up, you will be well paid.
If he can't get up, give him your blessing."
Then Umer the Sawsmith speaks out:
"Give me your black eyes, Angelina,
And I'll sharpen your Dojčin's sabre."
Angelina comes home, weeping and shrieking.
And cries out, "Bolen Dojčin!
Umer will not sharpen your sabre,
He refuses to do it on trust.
He wants my black eyes as his payment."
Bolen Dojčin gives her his answer:
"Leave the sabre, Angelina, my sister,
Let it lie here upon my white bed,
Go instead into my dark stable
And lead out my swift-footed horse.
Lead him down the road to the blacksmith,
To Mitré Pomoryanché,
To whom I am sworn as a brother.
Let him shoe my horse on trust.
If I get up, he will be well paid:
I will pay him in ducats of gold."
Then young Angelina stands up
And enters into the dark stable.
She leads out her brother's swift horse
And takes him to Mitré Pomoryanché

For him to shoe the horse on trust.
"By God's mercy, Mitré Pomoryanché,
If my Bolen Dojčin gets up
He will pay you for shoeing his horse."
But Mitré Pomoryanché says to her,
"Ah, so, my young Angelina,
If you give me your fair, lovely face,
Your face as bright as the sun,
Your eyebrows as black as sea leeches,
And your eyes like black grapes from the vines."
But the young Angelina cries out,
Beating her knees with her fists
And the tears streaming down her fair cheeks,
From her cheeks to her embroidered bodice,
From her bodice to her richly sewn skirt,
From her skirt onto the rough ground.
While leading her Dojčin's horse homeward
Angelina cries out bitter curses:
"May God kill you, Mitré Pomoryanché!
Why did you not strike with your sword,
And slay me rather than shame me?"
She comes home and says to her brother,
"And so, my own Bolen Dojčin,
For your sake I have suffered great shame.
Your loyal sworn brother has shamed me,
You who feasted and drank wine together,
You who hunted the forests together.
When I asked him to shoe your horse,
When I asked him to shoe it on trust,
Mitré Pomoryanché told me,
"If you give me your fair, lovely face
Then I'll shoe Dojčin's horse on trust!"
Bolen Dojčin leaps from his sickbed
And stands on his hero's legs.
"So, Angelina, my sister,
Do not fear and do not be ashamed!
Only for me take out my cold weapons,

Give them to the braid-headed Pavlé.
So he can wash the cold weapons."
The young Angelina stands up,
And she carries her brother's cold weapons.
"So, Braid-headed Pavlé,
Will you wash for me these cold weapons?"
"So, O sister Angelina.
What good are these weapons to him
If your brother Dojčin is ailing?"
"The Black Arab has appeared below Solun,
He raised his white tents on the plains,
His tents on the meadows of Solun
And has gathered the elders and priests.
He demands as his tribute two ovens of bread,
One barrel of arak, two barrels of wine,
An uncalved heifer he demands,
Every day he demands a fair bride,
Every night he demands a young maiden
To love and then to destroy.
My turn has come; now they will take me."
Then braid-headed Pavlé says to her,
"Ah, so, my young Angelina,
If you give me your slender body,
Your body like seaside reeds,
I will wash for you these cold weapons."
She picks up Dojčin's cold weapons
And returns to her smooth courtyard.
"So, my brother, Bolen Dojčin,
You do not have loyal sworn brothers,
All of them are infidel Turks!
All he wanted was my slender body."
"So, Angelina, my sister!
May they perish, my loyal sworn brothers!
May the eating and drinking cease!
Unroll me that fine cotton cloth
To bind up my dagger wounds."
Angelina binds his dagger wounds

147

And hands him his cold weapons.
He winds on his long silken sash
And thrusts within the steel weapons.
Then he siezes his rusty sabre
And mounts his unshod horse.
He rides straight to Salonika town,
Straightaway he rides to the white tent
And dismounts from his swift horse,
And draws out his damascene[1] sabre.
Then he kills that black Arab,
And with him, the yellow Jew.
Then Dojčin remounts his swift horse
And he puts the head on his pommel
And rides through the center of Solun.
All who see him look in amazement:
"What could be that wonder of wonders.
that hero[2] as dry as a tree,
Whose face appears as strained wax,
What a wonder he has wrought!
He has been and will be a hero!
No churches does he need to build,
Monasteries he need not support."
He rides through the market center
And comes upon Umer the Sawsmith
"And so, O Umer the Sawsmith,
Why did you not sharpen my sabre on trust?
What do you demand of my sister?
Why do you demand her black eyes?"
Dojčin draws his damascene sabre
And takes off his head.
Then he rides to Mitré Pomoryanché.

---

1. In the original the adjective is properly translated as "folding." ED.
2. *Yunak,* a term for "warrior" or "hero" or "brave" (n.), implying approval and connoting sexual and physical prowess, is not fully translatable into English. It is rendered here as "hero." ED.

"So, Mitré Pomoryanché,
Pomoryanché, my sworn loyal brother,
Who was to me like my black eyes!
What is this great shame and disgrace
That you have brought down on my sister?"
And likewise takes off his head.
Then he rides on to braid-headed Pavlé
And likewise takes off his head.
He rides home and calls out from afar,
"Open up, Angelina, my sister,
Open you wide our high gates!
Lay my bed in the painted chamber,
Bring me all the oil lamps and candles,
Fetch me priests well versed in God's law.
What you wanted, my sister, I have done.
Now my soul is departing my body.
O sister, no sorrow nor tears!
Go hire musicians and singers
And prepare to give a great feast."[1]
His sister Angelina stands up
And opens wide their high gates,
She is frightened, terribly frightened.
When she sees the Black Arab's head,
She embraces her Bolen Dojčin
And leads him to the painted chamber.
As soon as he lies upon his soft bed
Bolen Dojčin gives us his soul.
While his sister is lighting a candle,
Bolen Dojčin gives up his soul.
The priests and the elders have gathered.
The hired musicians have entered,
And they play for three days and three nights.

translation by Eugene Prostov, Elisavietta Ritchie, and Graham W. Reid

---

1. Musicians and singers today are very much in evidence at a Macedonian wedding feast. ED.

Kraljević Marko Loses His Strength

1

My divine God, you my God,
Source of my wonder, my marvelous,
You astound all Christendom
That your name is divined,
Engendered from age to age.
Thank you for so great a wonder
As for us to see this truth.

2

Marko of Prilep with his might
Journeying across a cold country
High on a spotted horse,
The big beast rending the barren air.
He wears on his head a sable helmet
A helmet with three mirrors
Three mirrors and peacock plumes.
He has rolled his moustache of brown hair
That resembled three black shocks.
He squints his falcom eyes black
And his frown forms his leech-shaped eyebrows
Like the wide wings of the swallow.
The sabre buckled to his side
Can turn on itself twelve times
And can cut through trees and stones.
Strapped to his saddle, O earth,
A frightening mass of arms weighing
At least a hundred thousand pounds.
His war weapon is locked in his hand,

As we have seen, Prince Marko and his fabulous horse are figures of superhuman strength and intelligence. But God (or the gods, as the case may be) will deprive even Prince Marko of his powers if he becomes too proud. This example of epic narrative from the Marko cycle attests to that fact. ED.

A long lance lean like a poplar.
He is hugged by a great cape
That darkens him like the black cloud.
Where his huge horse plants his foot
Even on a stone or a rock
This heaving animal half sinks up to his knees.
What does one make of a hero's strength
That the black and maternal earth
Groans to support his enormous weight,
Groans, the black and wrinkled earth,
Groans and shudders like a beast?

3

The star of evening witnessed this wonder
A true wonder never before seen
Where Kraljević Marko journeys
Sweating from the weight of his strength
The strength he strains to understand.
He has no equal among heroes,
All heroes even villains
Nor among monsters nor the Hydra-headed serpents
Not even the elves and nymphs
Nor the flesh-fearing divinities of the forest.
Journeying Marko crossed the country,
A deserted and dismal land.
There is no one there to encounter,
No one to speak to, no one to negate.
Marko lifted his eyes toward the sky
And saw the stationary star
Twinkling, laughing in its own light.
Then Kraljević Marko spoke to the star:
"You up there, star of evening,
I must question you, speak to me!
I journey across this country
And I have no equal among heroes,
Among all heroes even villains

Nor among monsters nor the Hydra-headed serpents
Not even the elves and the nymphs.
You who shine on high, star above,
You who survey the sweep of things, speak to me,
Is there nobody as heroic as I am?"
"To you Kraljević Marko
I will speak to you the truth,
I who shine far above
Surveying the sweep of things,
I have never seen a hero like you,
There never was, there never will be."
Marko of Prilep, let God punish him
For having shouted those stupid words,
For having committed so great a folly
That the cost to him is to lose his strength.
"Well then, star of evening,
You still do not know of my prowess,
Listen to me well, star of evening,
If God descended from the height of the heavens
Even against him I would battle
And if our earth had a flange
With one hand I would seize it."
The star of evening listened to Marko
And the star replied nothing.
Her face shrunk into its own gloom,
All in a gloom all in a cloud.
Quickly she hid herself behind a cloud.
Because she was chagrined
She cried in her cloud
Her tears falling from above
Like a fine dew onto the ground.

4

Marko continued his journey
A journey into agony.
He had tired his huge horse

Who now stumbled among the stones and rocks.
Kraljević Marko had beaten him
Between his black eyes with his heavy arms.
But the brave animal revived,
The black and barren earth shuddered,
It groaned and grumbled, the black earth.
And the wild winds howled,
The lakes and the rivers began to swell,
The black seas began to dance
Away with the white foam.
The booming seas began to boil.
The mountains grumbled and heaved higher.
Men were frightened in their towns
As were the beasts at the bottom of their caves.
The little birds of the earth
Continually chirped their concern,
And their cries arrived at last to God.
Merciful God, He had listened well.
He looked toward the earth.
He saw the barren black earth
Groan and shudder like a beast.
The Eternal One took pity
Because He understood that the earth
Would not support so great a force.
Then from the sky He descended
Disguising Himself as an old man.
And He took a small sack
And filled the sack with earth.
Then He blessed it, once, twice,
And the small sack became heavy,
As heavy as our entire earth.
God set the sack down at a crossroads
Where Kraljević Marko would pass.
And soon Marko appeared
Leaping from mountain to mountain,
Before him only fog and dust

Behind him a spray of stones
Shooting from the hoofs of his great horse.
When the bold horse breathed
His nostrils spewed forth a flame
And from his snout swung a white foam,
A white foam streaked with his blood.
Then Kraljević Marko saw something
On the white road crossing the plain,
A bent old man coming toward him
Carrying on his back a small sack.
The old man had come to the crossroads
And he sat down there in order to rest.
Kraljević Marko then turned toward him
Speaking out at still some distance:
"Good evening, Grandfather! Old father,
What mind of misfortune makes you
Trudge along so, wasting time
To cross this deserted country
Carrying so small a sack?"
The old man then replied:
"Praise you, powerful man-dragon,
I reply to you all in truth.
I trudge along crossing this country
And I carry with me this small sack,
But it is heavy, too heavy for me,
So heavy. I can no longer lift it.
I beg you, brave young god,
Help me to lift just a little
This sack which I must set on my back."
Kraljević Marko smiled
As he assayed the small sack
Which the old man labored to carry.
He wielded his war lance
To lift the sack with the end of it.
Nothing happened, the sack did not budge.
He took the lance with both hands

Then braced himself to lift it,
But the lance broke in half.

Kraljević Marko shrunk in awe,
His mouth gaping, his eyes glaring in disbelief.
He urged nearer his huge horse
And leaned over toward the sack.
He reached out his right arm.
He tried to take hold of the small sack
To take hold of it with his small finger
To pull it straight upward.
The great horse heaved with one last breath
And out of breath, he said to Marko:
"Listen to me, my master,
You have cracked my bones
You have ripped my powerful veins
You have drained my strength."
When Marko turned to look at him
He saw an extraordinary sight.
His horse was up to his knees.
And still the small sack did not budge.
Kraljević Marko became enraged.
He dismounted from his horse.
With his right foot he kicked the sack
With all his mad strength.
Pain pierced his right foot.
Again the sack did not budge.
Marko became mad with rage.
He took the sack between his hands.
He pulled with all his wild strength.
Into the stone ground went his feet.
His face was running with the sweat
Of blood. His eyes were bulging
Ready to burst from his face.
As he clenched his teeth
His mouth filled with blood.

155

Then at last the sack budged.
With an immense new effort Marko lifted
The sack to the level of his elbow,
The height of his elbow above the earth,
All the while his legs thrust
Into the ground up to his knees.
Then the old man said to him:
"Well then, Kraljević Marko,
Do you know what weight you have just carried?"
And Kraljević Marko replied,
"Tell me, grandfather, old grandfather,
What kind of wonder is that here?
With what is this small sack filled?"
And the old man replied,
"Listen to me well, Kraljević Marko,
You have just lifted the entire earth.
Do you have enough strength left
To come and fight fairly
With the Great Lord of the skies?"
Then Kraljević Marko replied:
"By God's mercy what a miracle!
I have been made mad and stupid.
If I am unable to lift the sack
How will I fight well
With the Great God of the skies?"
Then the old man said to him:
"Listen to me well, Kraljević Marko,
When you pulled at the sack with your lance
Your lost half of your strength.
When you pulled at the sack with your finger
You lost a half of your remaining strength.
When you pulled at the sack with your hands
You lost yet another half.
When you finally lifted the sack
You lost your strength of your young years.
I now make you this gift to be henceforth

A new hero among heroes
Knowing there is always One stronger than you.
With only your strength you will not triumph
Over the unknown,
But you will come to know defeat
From dealing with guile and deception."
Having spoken, the old man disappeared.
Marko of Prilep, numbed into knowing,
Set out alone on the white road.
He no longer moved like a bold dragon.
He went gently, he went slowly,
The tears running down his pale cheeks.
He pressed his hands on his white knees.
He went lamenting the strength of his young years
The power he had lost.

To the town of Prilep he returned.
There as a young man he married.
He remained to protect his kingdom
To protect his country, his land.
And since that time, Kraljević Marko
Has had to struggle with deception.

5

These times have been, these times have past.
The custom is to sing of them,
To sing the past
Celebrating the sacred name of God.
Then all Christendom hears
For otherwise it would not be sung.
Those who have listened, let them be joyous.

translation by Harry Williams

Whose Is Yonder Girl?

Whose is yonder girl
Who goes early to the water,
Than all others earlier still,
Than the fairest of young brides,
Than the widows with dark eyes,
Who wears a ducat on her brow,
Who wears a feather in her cap?
She has loosed her hair upon her shoulders,
Pushed her cap up from her eye
To see the plain so wide.
The wide plain it is endless,
The high tree it is kinless,
The deep sea it is sightless,
The fine sand it is countless,
And the young girl she is kinless.

translation by Graham W. Reid

In 1861, with the assistance of Bishop Strossmayer, Dimitar and Konstantin Miladinov published in Zagreb a collection of folk songs and sayings from their native Struga and Kukuš. *Zbornik* ("Collection") as it was called, contained over seven hundred separate items, and it was significant as the first such collection of Macedonian folk literature. This song is taken from that collection. ED.

Appendix: Ancestors

Black Came the Plague

Black came the plague
Down there in Macedonia,
Down there at Demir Kapija.[1]
Who will be the hero
Who scatters the plague?
A hero is chosen, is found,
Young Delče, the young Leader.
He is come to Macedonia
To scatter far the plague.
A black cloud came up
Down there in Macedonia,
Down there at Demir Kapija.
Are those black clouds
Or are they pagan Turks?
Black clouds they are not
Nor yet pagan Turks;
They are a band of heroes,
They are the Leader's men.
Wounded they bear the hero,
The wounded hero, young Delče,
Young Delče, the young Leader.
Delče said to his band:
Faithful, sworn band,
Tomorrow you will go
Through our troubled land.
When you pass
Through Kukuš, my town,

At the end of the nineteenth century, with the resurgence of Macedonian nationalism, the traditions and forms of the folk epic were adapted for political purposes by folk singers and poets. This poem concerns Goce Delčev (1872–1903), a Macedonian revolutionary and nationalist, creator and leader of the Internal Macedonian Revolutionary Organization. ED.

1. Demir Kapija, lit., the Iron Gates, is a gorge on the River Vardar.

159

Appendix: Ancestors

My mother will wait for you
And she will ask of you:
Where is young Delče, my son?
You will say to her:
Young Delče is betrothed
To a maid, Macedonia,
Black Land of slavery.

translation by Graham W. Reid

BEFORE THE WAR:
THE BEGINNINGS OF A LITERARY POETRY

KONSTANTIN MILADINOV (1830–1862)

Longing for the South

If I had an eagle's wings,
I would raise myself and fly on them
To our shores—to Stamboul and Kukuš.
I would watch the sun; is it
As faded there as it is here?
If it's the same faded sun.

If it's the same sun as here,
I'd make another journey,
I'd go somewhere else,
Where a bright sun greets me,
Where the sky is strewn with stars.
Here I am in a circle of darkness.
Fog covers everything.
It's all blizzards and raw winds.
The fog covers me. The ground is ice.
My head is filled with the coldness.

I'm not going to stay here;
I can't stand looking at these dark frosts.
Give me the wings and I'll wear them;

Konstantin Miladinov's "T'ga za jug" ("Longing for the South") was probably written during the poet's sojourn in Moscow (1856–1860), where he was studying Slavonic philology and preparing the collection of folk poetry. "Longing for the South" is the best known work of this poet, whose handful of original verses mark the beginning of literary poetry in Macedonian. As one critic has it, "Those who composed poems before Konstantin were not true poets—they were simple writers of verse." ED.

I'll fly to our shores,
I'll come again to our places,
To Ohrid and to Struga,
Where the sun can warm the soul,
Where the bright sun sets in the forests,
Where nature gives you something—
Real gifts.
Where the lake can stretch out white,
Or the wind can darken it blue.
Look at these plains, these mountains—
God's beauty.
      There I can sing to my heart's content—
      Ah! Let the sun set! Let me die.

translation by Milne Holton and Graham W. Reid

Appendix: Ancestors

GRIGOR PRLIČEV (1830/31–1882)

From *Scanderbeg*

Among them they saw Scanderbeg, all powerful
As Ares, his sword high and dripping
With warm blood, their crazed minds unloosed
By the fear in their burning hearts.
Shefia was the first slain, their leader,
Empowered over half of all their foot soldiers,
Taking the metal between his brows
And in the brain; then there was Sheid,
Struck through the left breast, the sword
Finding an easy exit beneath the shoulder blade.
But Scanderbeg pulled it free with one stroke
And Sheid fell like a log to the earth
Full on his forehead; then the great Shakir

Grigor Prličev, during his medical student days in Athens, composed—in Greek—two heroic narrative poems. The first, *The Sirdar* (1860), won first prize in a traditional poetry competion sponsored by the Greek prince, Otto. The second, written the following year, was *Scanderbeg*. But after the deaths of the Miladinov brothers in a jail in Constantinople in 1862, Prličev returned to Ohrid to continue their work. In 1871 he began translating his two poems—along with the *Iliad* and *Orlando Furioso*—into his own "Pan-Slavonic" language. These translations have become foundation blocks for modern Macedonian poetry. *The Sirdar* was translated into English by Graham W. and Peggy Reid and published in Skopje in 1973. See T. Spasov's afternote in their *The Sirdar* (Skopje: Macedonian Review Editions, 1973), pp. 73–89, 87. Scanderbeg (Skanderbeg, Iskander, or Alexander Bey), whose real name was George Castriota (1403–1468), led a national uprising of Albanians against the Turks in 1443 and, with Venetian and Neapolitan help, maintained Albanian independence for some twenty years. He is today Albania's national hero, and Scanderbeg legends find a sympathetic audience among Macedonians as well.
The selection here translated is from section IV, ll. 2628–73.

163

And proud Issac were set free in death;
Shakir's head fell first, then the left arm
Lopped off from the shoulder;
Then Husnia, Ahmed's brave brother,
Who once came as commander to Cruia
At the head of twelve thousand troops,
Caught in the bloody fight against Scanderbeg,
He who butchered thousands with his own hands
And as booty took back the rest alive,
Against Scanderbeg now; and mules too,
Sent into Cruia bearing on their backs
Loads of silver as ransom for prisoners.
As the north wind drives the rain clouds
Brought to swelling by the south wind
To caulk the star-holed sky,
So did he rend the enemy's ranks,
Savage Scanderbeg, ceaseless, slaying
All that stood before his wildness;
As fast as the rain falls he destroyed the Turks,
Heaping high the corpses of the troops
Into a space eight yards square or more.
The Pasha was gone, then did he cast out his iron glance,
Intimidating the entire enemy;
He relished the sight of his two captains,
Crnoević, terror to the Turks, and Andreia Topia,
Both with their blood-wet hands
Towering over the warriors like oaks of the forest,
Routing the enemy's wedged-in ranks
Fighting without fear of their flesh,
Soul suffused, so that they excelled.
His eyes burning and with a flaming face
He bellowed like a raging bull,
He derided the fallen, he cried out without measure;
He drew strength from his derision of the slain;
Yet Crnoević showed grace in the savage struggle,

Appendix: Ancestors

A coolness that allowed him his smile
As the lover smiles at the wedding feast
When he catches the eye of his beloved.

imitation by Harry Williams from a translation by Graham W. Reid of M. D.
Petruševski's Macedonian rendering of the Greek original

Appendix: Ancestors

KOSTA SOLEV RACIN (1908–1943)

From *Elegies for You*

Darken, forest, darken, sister . . . !   Folk Song

1

Yesterday I walked
Through that green woodland
Beneath those tall trees
In the shadows on the ground.

I was in a trance,
Nodding, listless,
And as I walked, my heart
Felt like some dark stone in my breast.

Forest full of heroes,
Cool streams for the heroes,

"Kočo" Racin is today very much the embodiment of the partizan poet, a kind of folk hero for contemporary Macedonians. Born to a carpenter's family, he was from his early years associated with progressive movements; much of his short life was spent in prisons, and he died as a partizan in the hills of Macedonia. His surviving literary output is slight; like many of his manuscripts, his only novel, *Afion* ("Opium Poppy"), was destroyed by the police, but his one collection of twelve poems, *Beli Mugri* ("White Dawns," 1939), survives to suggest something of his intense social awareness and his deep response to his natural environment, qualities which shaped much of the poetry written in Macedonia immediately after the war.

White Dawns stands as an historical monument as well. The collection represents one of the first attempts at literary expression in "modern Macedonian," a literary language which has previously existed only as the theoretical construction of Krsté Misirkov (in his *Za makedonskite raboti,* or "Concerning the Macedonian Question." 1903), but which would go on to become the basis for the ultimate resolution of dialectal differences and the foundation for the official literary language. Thus, *White Dawns* is in several senses the first collection of modern Macedonian poetry. ED.

Though the birds sing, you are crying.
And though the sun is shining, all you see is darkness.

What if you hide the bones
Of those brave young men,
Scattered here in the shadows
Of your trees?

But why conceal their songs?
Why do the trees,
Even their branches,
Even their leaves,
Seem to be whispering some sad secret?

. . . .

4

The life of a worker is the life of a beast
Walled in by the darkness;
We are forced to become beasts
In this fine world.

Who caused our wings to be broken,
Our frail, white, dove wings?
Who muddied the water,
The clear springs of our souls?

And who separated man from man
With these walls?
And why must one man
Be slave to another?

Man is separated from men,
And suffers
And crawls,
And is forced to flee—
From birth to death.

imitation by Peter Van Egmond from a translation by Graham W. Reid

The Poets

CANÉ ANDREEVSKI. Cané Andreevski was born in Kratovo in 1930 and presently resides in Skopje, where he works for Skopje Radio-TV. A journalist and a children's writer, he was also published five collections of poems, all of which have been widely translated and well received throughout eastern Europe.

PETRÉ M. ANDREEVSKI. Petré M. Andreevski, born in 1934 in the village of Sloeśtica, has been publishing collections of his poetry since 1960. Full recognition of his importance came in 1971, however, when "Death of the Guiser" won the prize for the best Macedonian poem of the year at the Struga Poetry Festival.

PETRÉ BAKEVSKI. One of the youngest of the poets here represented, Petré Bakevski was born in 1947 in Kavadarci, one of Macedonia's most important wine-producing towns. A journalist as well as a poet, Bakevski's first collection of poems appeared in 1972.

JOZO T. BOŠKOVSKI. Jozo T. Boškovski was born in 1933 in the village of Ostrilci and graduated from the University of Skopje. He has published art criticism, essays, and several collections of poetry.

PETAR BOŠKOVSKI. Petar Boškovski was also born in Ostrilci, in 1936. Now he lives in Skopje and is the editor of *Razgledi* ("Vistas"), a leading literary journal in Macedonia. He is regarded as one of the most vigorous and authentic of his generation of poets.

KIRIL BUJUKLIEV. Kiril Bujukliev, born in 1937 in Štip, is a working journalist in Skopje. His first volume of poems was published in 1968.

VERA BUŽAROVSKA. Vera Bužarovska was born in Bitola in 1931 and began writing in the late 1950s. She writes for children, but her adult fiction and poetry has also received attention. Her most recent collection of poems appeared in 1972.

TODOR ČALOVSKI. Born in 1946 in Galičnik, Todor Čalovski lives and works in Skopje. Presently he is employed as a critic for Skopje Radio-TV. Two books of his poems have so far been published.

RADOVAN P. CVETKOVSKI. When Radovan Cvetkovski's *Moeto podnebje* ("My Clime") was published in Bitola in 1971, this first collection by a young poet caused an immediate literary sensation. The poems flew in the face of the new international trends of Macedonian poetry by returning to an intensely localized imagery. The poem in our anthology was taken from that collection.

BOGOMIL GJUZEL. Bogomil Gjuzel was born in Čačak in 1939. Educated at the University of Skopje and at Edinburgh, he now lives in Skopje with his British wife. He has been employed as a literary editor, as a director of repertory at the Dramatic Theatre in Skopje, as an official of the Writers' Union, and as a festival director. Known primarily as a poet with several acclaimed collections to his credit, Gjuzel is also an established playwright and author of short stories. He spent 1972–1973 in residence at the Iowa International Writers' Workshop. At present he is back in Skopje and is devoting full time to his writing.

SVETLANA HRISTOVA-JOCIĆ. Svetlana Hristova was born in Resen in 1941 and is now married and living in Skopje. She has published her poetry in three collections to date, the first, *Kalesnica,* appearing in 1970.

SRBO IVANOVSKI. Srbo Ivanovski was born at Štip in 1928 and now lives in Skopje. He is best known as a lyricist, having published his first collections of poems as early as 1950. But he has also anthologized Macedonian poetry.

ČEDO JAKIMOVSKI. Čedo Jakimovski was born in Kratovo in 1940 and now lives in Skopje, where he edits a journal.

SLAVKO JANEVSKI. Slavko Janevski, one of Macedonian's best regarded and most prolific writers, was born in Skopje in 1920, where he is presently living. He fought as a partizan during the war, wrote the first full-length novel in Macedonian, *Selo zad sedumte jesenu* ("The Village Behind the Seven Aspens," 1952), and has been widely translated as a poet. Janevski is actively involved in the academic and publishing worlds of Skopje.

BLAŽE KONESKI. Blaže Koneski was born near Prilep in 1921. He is known as a linguist as well as a poet, having been largely responsible for the standardization of modern literary Macedonian and having published one of the first collections of poetry, *Zemjata i lubovta* ("Land and Love," 1948) in the Macedonian language after the war. He presently lives in Skopje, where he is President of the Macedonian Aca-

The Poets

demy of Arts and Sciences and former Rector (President) of Cyril and Methodius University.

JOVAN KOTEVSKI. Jovan Kotevski was born in Prisovjani village, near Ohrid, in 1935. He has been publishing collections of his poetry since 1958.

MATEJA MATEVSKI. Mateja Matevski was born in Istanbul in 1929 and now lives on the side of Mt. Nerezi, in the suburbs of Skopje. Matevski began his writing career in 1956; today he is one of Macedonia's most respected poets. He also serves as General Director of Skopje Radio-TV.

RADOVAN PAVLOVSKI. Radovan Pavlovski, born in Niš in 1937, studied law at the University of Skopje. He published four collections of his poetry in Macedonian and quickly came to be recognized as one of the region's most exciting if most disturbing poets. He now lives near Zagreb and is writing in Croatian as well as in Macedonian.

ANTÉ POPOVSKI. Anté Popovski was born in Lazaropolé in 1931. He now lives in Skopje, where he is director of a publishing house.

MIHAIL RENDŽOV. Born in Štip in 1936, Mihail Rendžov began publishing his poems in collections in 1964. His reputation is a recent one, however, and the attention to his poems has been a phenomenon of recent years.

JOVAN STREZOVSKI. Jovan Strezovski was born in Podgorci village, near Struga, and began publishing his poetry in the late 1950s. Since then some nine collections of his poems have appeared. His novel, *Voda* ("Water") of 1972 achieved critical acclaim, but Strezovski remains best known as a poet.

ACO ŠOPOV. Aco Šopov, one of Macedonia's most widely translated and most admired poets, was born in Štip in 1923 and now lives in Skopje. He published his first collection of poetry in 1944 and has since been recognized as the leader of the subjectivist poets.

DUŠICA TODOROVSKA. Born in 1944, Dušica Todorovska has published her poems in two collections, appearing in 1971 and 1974. She

171

presently resides in Skopje and is regarded as a distinguished example of the new breed of young women writers.

GANÉ TODOROVSKI. Born in 1929 in Skopje, where he now lives and teaches, Gané Todorovski has published at last count six collections of his remarkable poetry. He is also an established Slavic literary historian and one of his university's most distinguished teachers.

VLADA UROŠEVIĆ. Vlada Urošević, born in Skopje in 1934, still makes his home there. He has been publishing his collections and anthologies since 1959, and is recognized as the leader of the "internationalist" group of Macedonian poets. He works for Skopje Radio-TV.

ATANAS VANGELOV. Atanas Vangelov, one of Macedonia's most exciting younger poets, was born in 1946 in Bogdanci. He began publishing his poems in 1966 and has since been the object of attention of serious readers of Macedonian poetry.

The Translators

VERA BUŽAROVSKA. Vera Bužarovska appears in this anthology as one of the New Poets.

DANICA CVETANOVSKA. Danica Cvetanovska has studied in the United States. She now lives and teaches in her native city, Skopje.

VLADO CVETKOVSKI. Vlado Cvetkovski, having recently returned after a Fulbright year in the United States, now resides in Skopje (not far from his native Bitola), where he teaches in the English Department at Cyril and Methodius University.

ANN DARR. Ann Darr lives in Chevy Chase, Maryland. She is a pilot of airplanes as well as a poet. Her 1971 collection, *St. Ann's Gut,* was nationally acclaimed, and her most recent collection, *The Myth of a Woman's Fist,* appeared in 1975.

BILJANA DIMOVSKA. Biljana Dimovska, a recent graduate of Skopje University, lives in Skopje and works there as a translator.

HOWARD ERSKINE-HILL. Howard Erskine-Hill is well known as a translator of Slavic writers in Britain. Also a student of the poetry of Alexander Pope, he has published an edition of Pope's *The Dunciad* (1972).

ROLAND FLINT. Roland Flint presently lives in Georgetown, D.C., and teaches creative writing at Georgetown University. His poems have appeared widely in journals and have been collected in his *And Morning* (1975).

MARGARET GIBSON. Margaret Gibson is now living and writing in Connecticut. Her poems and short stories have appeared in various journals.

BOGOMIL GJUZEL. Bogomil Gjuzel appears in this anthology as one of the Avant-Garde.

EDWARD GOLD. Edward Gold lives and writes poetry in Washington, D.C., and teaches at the University of Maryland. He is a graduate of Elliott Coleman's writers' program at the Johns Hopkins University.

The Translators

DANIEL HOFFMAN. Daniel Hoffman, poet and professor of American literature, lives in Swarthmore and teaches at the University of Pennsylvania. He has completed a tenure as Poetry Consultant at the Library of the Congress in Washington. His most recent critical book, entitled *Poe Poe Poe Poe Poe Poe* (1972) is, curiously enough, a study of Edgar Allan Poe. His most recent collection of poems is *The Center of Attention* (1974).

RODERICK JELLEMA. Roderick Jellema, a poet and teacher, lives in Takoma Park, Maryland, and teaches at the University of Maryland. *Something Tugging the Line,* a collection of his poems, appeared in 1974.

CAROLYN KIZER. Carolyn Kizer is presently Visiting Professor of Poetry at the University of Maryland. She is the author of several books of poetry, including the recent *Midnight Was My Cry* (1971).

IVANKA KOVILOSKA-POPOSKA. Ivanka Koviloska-Poposka, having recently returned from a Visiting Lectureship in Macedonian and Serbo-Croatian at the University of Bradford, is again teaching in the Department of English at the University of Skopje; she has studied in both the United States and Britain, and her translations appear regularly in Macedonian journals.

HERBERT KUHNER. Herbert Kuhner is an American writer living in Vienna. His first novel, *Nixe,* appeared in 1968; he has recently completed another and is presently at work on a play. His translations and poems have appeared in various journals.

B. KUNOVSKA. B. Kunovska is a recent graduate of the Cyril and Methodius University, Skopje, where she is now living.

NANCY MARKS. Nancy Marks, who has published poems in various periodicals, is presently a student of architecture at the University of Michigan.

ARVIND KRISHNA MEHROTRA. Arvind Krishna Mehrotra, who spent the year of 1972–1973 in residence at the Iowa International Writers' Workshop, has returned to his native India, where he teaches English at the University of Allahabad.

The Translators

VASA D. MIHAILOVICH. Vasa D. Mihailovich teaches Slavic languages and literature at the University of North Carolina. He has recently co-edited *An Introduction to Yugoslav Literature* (1973) with Branko Mikasinovich and Dragan Milivojevic, and he is presently at work on a bibliography of Yugoslav literature in translation.

LENA OGNENOVA. Lena Ognenova, a graduate of Skopje University, now lives in Skopje and is employed as a professional translator.

LINDA PASTAN. Linda Pastan lives in Rockville, Maryland. She has two books of poetry, *A Perfect Circle of Sun* (1971) and *On the Way to the Zoo* (1975).

EUGENE PROSTOV. Eugene Prostov, who was born in Russia and raised in Bulgaria, now lives in Washington, D.C. He has recently retired after a distinguished career in government service; his last position was with the United States Information Agency.

HEDDY REID. Heddy Reid lives in Washington, D.C., where she writes poetry. She reads her poems frequently before Washington audiences.

ELISAVIETTA RITCHIE. Elisavietta Ritchie, a writer and translator, is presently living in Washington, D.C. She has translated from the poetry of Aleksandr Blok; the most recent collection of her own poetry is *Tightening the Circle Over Eel Country* (1974).

CHARLES SIMIC. Charles Simic, who was born in Belgrade, lives in Northwood, New Hampshire, and teaches at the University of New Hampshire. His own poetry is widely published and much admired, but he is also known as a translator, one recent effort being the poems of the Serbian poet, Vasko Popa (*The Little Box*, 1970). His own most recent collection, *Return to a Place Lit by a Glass of Milk*, was published by Braziller early last year.

MYRA SKLAREW. Myra Sklarew lives in Bethesda, Maryland, and teaches poetry at American University in Washington, D.C. Her first book of poems, *From the Backyard of the Diaspora*, appeared in 1975.

KATICA TODOROVSKA. Katica Todorovska is a recent graduate of Cyril and Methodius University; she works in Skopje as a translator.

175

DUŠKO TOMOVSKI. Duško Tomovski, a professor of Germanic philology at Cyril and Methodius University, Skopje, was born in Debar in 1925. In addition to his academic accomplishments, Professor Tomovski is well known as a translator from English, French, and German literatures.

PETER VAN EGMOND. Peter Van Egmond lives in Upper Marlboro, Maryland, and teaches poetry at the University of Maryland. He has published his poems in various journals and has recently completed a bibliographical and critical study, *The Critical Reception of Robert Frost.*

REED WHITTEMORE. Reed Whittemore, former editor of *Furioso,* former literary editor of *The New Republic,* and a widely published poet in his own right, now lives in Washington, D.C., and teaches modern literature at the University of Maryland. His own most recent collection is entitled *Fifty Poems Fifty* and appeared in 1970. He has also recently completed a critical book, *William Carlos Williams* (1975).

HARRY WILLIAMS. A poet and critic, Harry Williams teaches literature at Riyadh University in Saudi Arabia. His essays and poems have appeared in various journals, and his critical study of the long poems of Theodore Roethke will soon be published by the Bucknell University Press. When not in Riyadh he lives on the Cornish coast with his wife, Lorna, who is a potter.

JOHN WOODBRIDGE. An architect and city planner, and a translator of poetry only by avocation, John Woodbridge lives in Washington, D.C. with his wife, Carolyn Kizer.

Pitt Poetry Series

Dannie Abse, *Collected Poems*   Cloth, ISBN 0-8229-3333-2, $9.95/Paper, ISBN 0-8229-5276-2, $3.95

Adonis, *The Blood of Adonis*   Cloth, ISBN 0-8229-3213-X $6.95/Paper, ISBN 0-8229-5220-3, $2.95

Jack Anderson, *The Invention of New Jersey*   Cloth, ISBN 0-8229-3168-0, $6.95/Paper, ISBN 0-8229-5203-3, $2.95

Jon Anderson, *Death & Friends*   Cloth, ISBN 0-8229-3202-4, $6.95/Paper ISBN 0-8229-5217-3, $2.95

Jon Anderson, *In Sepia*   Cloth, ISBN 0-8229-3278-4, $6.95/Paper, ISBN 0-8229-5245-9, $2.95

Jon Anderson, *Looking for Jonathan*   Cloth, ISBN 0-8229-3141-9, $6.95/Paper, ISBN 0-8229-5139-8, $2.95

John Balaban, *After Our War*   Paper, ISBN 0-8229-5247-5, $2.95

Gerald W. Barrax, *Another Kind of Rain*   Cloth, ISBN 0-8229-3206-7, $6.95/Paper, ISBN 0-8229-5218-1, $2.95

Leo Connellan, *First Selected Poems*   Paper, ISBN 0-8229-5268-8, $2.95

Michael Culross, *The Lost Heroes*   Paper, ISBN 0-8229-5251-3, $2.95

Fazıl Hüsnü Dağlarca, *Selected Poems*   Paper, ISBN 0-8229-5204-1, $2.95

James Den Boer, *Learning the Way*   Cloth, ISBN 0-8229-3140-0, $6.95/Paper, 0-8229-5138-X, $2.95

James Den Boer, *Trying to Come Apart*   Cloth, ISBN 0-8229-3216-4, $6.95/Paper, ISBN 0-8229-5221-1, $2.95

Norman Dubie, *Alehouse Sonnets*   Cloth, ISBN 0-8229-3226-1, $6.95/Paper, ISBN 0-8229-5223-8, $2.95

Norman Dubie, *In the Dead of the Night*   Paper, ISBN 0-8229-5261-0, $2.95

Odysseus Elytis, *The Axion Esti*   Cloth, ISBN 0-8229-3283-0, $7.50/Paper, ISBN 0-8229-5252-1, $3.50

John Engels, *Blood Mountain*   Cloth, ISBN 0-8229-3338-1, $6.95/Paper, ISBN 0-8229-5277-7, $2.95/Limited Edition, ISBN 0-8229-3289-X, $30.00

John Engels, *The Homer Mitchell Place*   Cloth, ISBN 0-8229-3149-4, $6.95/Paper, ISBN 0-8229-5159-2, $2.95

John Engels, *Signals from the Safety Coffin*   Cloth, ISBN 0-8229-3291-1, $6.95/Paper, ISBN 0-8229-5255-6, $2.95

Abbie Huston Evans, *Collected Poems*   ISBN 0-8229-3208-3, $7.95

Brendan Galvin, *No Time for Good Reasons*   Paper, ISBN 0-8229-5250-5, $2.95

Gary Gildner, *Digging for Indians*   Cloth, ISBN 0-8229-3230-X, $6.95/Paper, ISBN 0-8229-5224-6, $2.95

Gary Gildner, *First Practice*   Cloth, ISBN 0-8229-3179-6, $6.95/Paper, ISBN 0-8229-5208-4, $2.95

Gary Gildner, *Nails*   Cloth, ISBN 0-8229-3293-8, $6.95/Paper ISBN 0-8229-5257-2, $2.95

Mark Halperin, *Backroads*   Cloth, ISBN 0-7229-3311-X, $6.95/Paper, ISBN 0-8229-5266-1, $2.95

Michael S. Harper, *Dear John, Dear Coltrane*   Paper, ISBN 0-8229-5213-0, $2.95

Michael S. Harper, *Song: I Want a Witness*   Cloth, ISBN 0-8229-3254-7, $6.95/Paper, ISBN 0-8229-5231-9, $2.95

Samuel Hazo, *Blood Rights*   Cloth, ISBN 0-8229-3147-8, $6.95/Paper, ISBN 0-8229-5157-6, $2.95

Samuel Hazo, *Once for the Last Bandit: New and Previous Poems*   ISBN 0-8229-3240-7, $6.95

Samuel Hazo, *Quartered*   Cloth, ISBN 0-8229-3284-9, $6.95/Paper, ISBN 0-8229-5253-X, $2.95

Gwen Head, *Special Effects*   Paper, ISBN 0-8229-5258-0, $2.95

Milne Holton and Graham W. Reid, eds., *Reading the Ashes: An Anthology of the Poetry of Modern Macedonia*   Cloth, ISBN 0-8229-3337-3, $8.95/Paper, ISBN 0-8229-5282-3, $3.50

Shirley Kaufman, *The Floor Keeps Turning*   ISBN 0-8229-3190-7, $6.95

Shirley Kaufman, *Gold Country*   Cloth, ISBN 0-8229-3269-5, $6.95/Paper, ISBN 0-8229-5238-6, $2.95

Pitt Poetry Series

Abba Kovner, *A Canopy in the Desert: Selected Poems*   Cloth, ISBN 0-8229-3260-1, $8.95/Paper, ISBN 0-8229-5232-7, $3.95

Paul-Marie Lapointe, *The Terror of the Snows: Selected Poems*   Cloth, ISBN 0-8229-3327-6, $7.95/Paper, ISBN 0-8229-5274-2, $2.95

Larry Levis, *Wrecking Crew*   Cloth, ISBN 0-8229-3238-5, $6.95/Paper, ISBN 0-8229-5226-2, $2.95

Jim Lindsey, *In Lieu of Mecca*   Paper, ISBN 0-8229-5267-X, $2.95

Tom Lowenstein, tr., *Eskimo Poems from Canada and Greenland*   ISBN 0-8229-1110-8, $6.95

Archibald MacLeish, *The Great American Fourth of July Parade*   Paper, ISBN 0-8229-5272-6, $3.95/Record, $5.95

Judith Minty, *Lake Songs and Other Fears*   Paper, ISBN 0-8229-5242-4, $2.95

James Moore, *The New Body*   Paper, ISBN 0-8229-5260-2, $2.95

Carol Muske, *Camouflage*   Paper, ISBN 0-8229-5259-0, $2.95

Thomas Rabbit, *Exile*   Cloth, ISBN 0-8229-3292-X, $6.95/Paper, ISBN 0-8229-5256-4, $2.95

Belle Randall, *101 Different Ways of Playing Solitaire and Other Poems*   Cloth, ISBN 0-8229-3261-X, $6.95/Paper, ISBN 0-8229-5235-1, $2.95

Ed Roberson, *Etai-Eken*   Paper, ISBN 0-8229-5263-9, $2.95

Ed Roberson, *When Thy King Is A Boy*   Cloth, ISBN 0-8229-3197-4, $6.95/Paper, ISBN 0-8229-5214-9, $2.95

Eugene Ruggles, *The Lifeguard in the Snow*   Cloth, ISBN 0-8229-3336-5, $6.95/Paper, ISBN 0-8229-5281-5, $2.95/Limited Edition, ISBN 0-8229-3340-3, $30.00

Dennis Scott, *Uncle Time*   Cloth, ISBN 0-8229-3217-7, $6.95/Paper, ISBN 0-8229-5240-8, $2.95

Herbert Scott, *Disguises*   Paper, ISBN 0-8229-5248-3, $2.95

Herbert Scott, *Groceries*   Cloth, ISBN 0-8229-3332-2, $6.95/Paper, ISBN 0-8229-5270-X, $2.95

Richard Shelton, *Of All the Dirty Words*   Cloth, ISBN 0-8229-3248-2, $6.95/Paper, ISBN 0-8229-5230-0, $2.95

Richard Shelton, *The Tattooed Desert*   Cloth, ISBN 0-8229-3212-1, $6.95/Paper, ISBN 0-8229-5219-X, $2.95

Richard Shelton, *You Can't Have Everything*   Cloth, ISBN 0-8229-3309-8, $6.95/Paper, ISBN 0-8229-5262-9, $2.95

Gary Soto, *The Elements of San Joaquin*   Cloth, ISBN 0-8229-3335-7, $6.95/Paper, ISBN 0-8229-5279-3, $2.95/Limited Edition, ISBN 0-8229-3339-X, $30.00

David Steingass, *American Handbook*   Cloth, ISBN 0-8229-3270-9, $6.95/Paper, ISBN 0-8229-5239-4, $2.95

David Steingass, *Body Compass*   Cloth, ISBN 0-8229-3180-X, $6.95/Paper, ISBN 0-8229-5209-2, $2.95

Tomas Tranströmer, *Windows & Stones: Selected Poems*   Cloth, ISBN 0-8229-3241-5, $6.95/Paper, ISBN 0-8229-5228-9, $2.95

Alberta T. Turner, *Learning to Count*   Paper, ISBN 0-8229-5249-1, $2.95

Marc Weber, *48 Small Poems*   Cloth, ISBN 0-8229-3257-1, $6.95/Paper, ISBN 0-8229-5234-3, $2.95

David P. Young, *Sweating Out the Winter*   Paper, ISBN 0-8229-5172-X, $2.95

All prices are subject to change without notice. Order from your bookstore or the publisher.

University of Pittsburgh Press
Pittsburgh, Pa. 15260